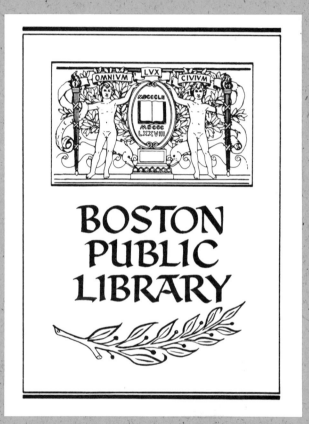

The
Night
Hank
Williams
Died

PLAYS BY LARRY L. KING

The Best Little Whorehouse in Texas (1977)

The Kingfish (1979)

The Night Hank Williams Died (1985)

Christmas: 1933 (1986)

The Golden Shadows Old West Museum (1987)

Produced on the New York stage
by Drew Dennett

Originally produced in New York City
by the WPA Theatre, 1989
(Kyle Renick, Artistic Director)

First professional production
at New Playwrights' Theatre
of Washington, D.C.
(Peter Frisch, Artistic Director,
Catherine M. Wilson, Managing Director)

The Night Hank Williams Died *contains no character purporting to be, or to represent or to be based on, the late country-western singing star; nor is this play in any way intended to be a representation of the life of Hank Williams. Indeed, it is set in West Texas in the summer of 1952, some six months before Hank Williams actually died in the back of an automobile near Oak Hill, West Virginia. The title is, therefore, intended to be purely symbolic.*

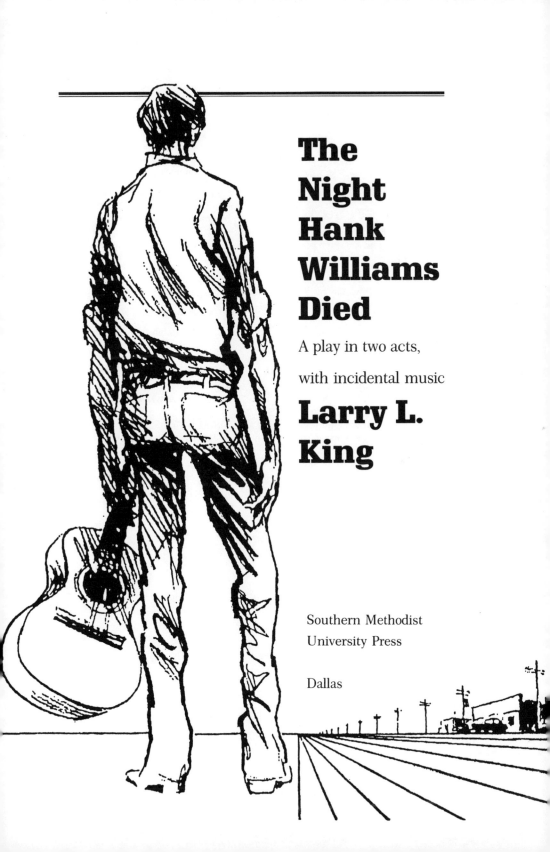

The Night Hank Williams Died

A play in two acts,

with incidental music

Larry L. King

Southern Methodist
University Press

Dallas

Stock royalty quoted on application to Samuel French, Inc.

The songs "A Slow Waltz in Time," "Sweet Precious Jesus," "Waking Up with Strangers," and "Yesterday Seemed Too Early" are © 1989 by Texhouse Corporation. Lyrics and music by Larry L. King.

Cover and title page illustration by Oliphant © 1987

Book Design by Richard Hendel

Cataloging-in-Publication Data

King, Larry L.
    The night Hank Williams died : a play in two acts, with incidental music / by Larry L. King.
        p.   cm.
    ISBN 0-87074-292-2. —
ISBN 0-87074-303-1 (pbk.)
    I. Title.
    PS3561.I48N5   1989
    812'.54—dc20   89-42894
                                              CIP

This book is for those who

helped to advance my play most:

Keith Kennedy, Peter Frisch,

Kyle Renick, Drew Dennett

and, of course, all the players

onstage in Memphis, Washington,

Austin and New York

Preface

The Night Hank Williams Died is a play from my blood; it is from what my friend and fellow writer Larry McMurtry has called "my blood's country and my heart's pastureland."

By that I mean the play's characters literally contain bits and pieces of my family as well as shavings and splinters of myself. "My blood's country and my heart's pastureland" is the setting of this play: that wind-blasted, sand-blown, baking-hot, high-skied and bone-lonesome endless reach of West Texas where in the 1940s and 1950s I was first a youthful would-be football hero, reluctant oil-patch rig hand and hopeful young newspaper reporter.

Many a shaping hour did I spend in dingy old beer joints much like Gus Gilbert's grandly named Sundowner Recreational Club in this play, joints where working people congregated ostensibly to party up a good time, but where—I then sometimes suspected and now devoutly believe—they most probably came to ease pain and escape loneliness. I dreamed varied dreams in such watering holes, to the accompaniment of jangling guitars and whining fiddles; none was more persistent than my dream of escaping that land which had nurtured me, however roughly. It is a grand irony that, once escaped, I have spent my life writing about the people, places and things I so long sought to flee. Perhaps it is my way of trying to define them and understand them.

It is difficult to know when or how one really begins an act of artistic creation. My first conscious awareness of this play traces to a young man's voice suddenly saying in my head, "I ain't got a dime, Gus. If they was givin' away free tumbleweeds, I couldn't afford the wind to get mine home." I have no idea where that voice came from or why it chose to speak as I walked down Connecticut Avenue in downtown Washington at midday in the summer of 1984, but I have no doubt I clearly heard it or that it spoke in that flat, twangy accent so indigenous to home. Clearly, it was a voice that might have more to say; I stopped walking and hastily scrawled that first bit of dialogue before continuing on to Duke Zeibert's restaurant for lunch.

In the next few months, as I worked on other writing projects, I periodically rescued that scrawled scrap from its assigned territory in the usual mound of desk litter and stared at it while wondering, *Who said that? And why? And who in the world is Gus?* One morning I decided to find out, and rolled a sheet of typing paper into my outmoded old Smith-Corona.

All I knew was that the scrap of dialogue seemed somehow to vaguely match up with an old, half-formed notion I long had harbored about one day writing a play in which country music would be used to assist the moods of various scenes and also to cover scene changes during stage blackouts. And so I opened with a young man, badly in need of a drink, carrying a guitar as he stumbled into a scruffy West Texas beer joint. It quickly developed that the beer joint was owned by an irascible old coot named Gus Gilbert and that he and the young man—Thurmond Stottle—were replaying a familiar scene between them, one in which Thurmond has to pay for a "free" beer by suffering yet another lecture from Gus about wasting his life in a nowhere town. A mutual dependency develops. Thurmond needs Gus as a source of emergency beer and small-sums loans between meager paydays, and to serve as a sounding board for his wild dream of becoming a country-western singing star ("the next Hank Williams") as well as to tolerate his beery, oft-told tales of having been a hotshot high school football hero, Thurmond's only time of glory in a life of tedium and hardscrabble. Mired in the present, Thurmond is sustained only by yesterday's memories and vain dreams of an impossible tomorrow made believable in his own mind with the assistance of alcohol. Gus, in the winter of his discontent, needs Thurmond as a surrogate to relive his own failed life and do a bit more with it than has Gus, who has come upon that time of life when one regrets not having risked the full adventure of one's self. And Gus also needs Thurmond because the latter is of such malleable clay, Gus having a tendency to command and manipulate.

That initial exploration of unknown fictional territory in time turned into what would become Act One, Scene One of *The Night*

Hank Williams Died. In the numerous rewrites of the play since my first rough draft was completed in May of 1985, many things have changed. I started with a cast of fourteen characters; they were whittled, by degrees, to eleven, then nine, then eight and finally to six characters. Much of the cutting reflected a practical need to reduce the cast size if one hoped to receive commercial productions; some had to do with honing and sharpening relationships between a manageable number of characters. For those reasons three rowdy oil-field workers, a lonely and drunk Air Force "fly-boy," the husband of Nellie Bess, two tourists from Ohio and the local financial patriarch—Tood Brandon—eventually disappeared, though Tood Brandon remains an offstage presence and vital to the plot. Nellie Bess's husband, Howard, was replaced by a persistent, offstage car horn. The horn worked cheaper.

But very little has been changed from the original writing in the play's opening scene between Thurmond and Gus; their relationship was pretty much defined in my first crack at it. At the end of that scene, however, I had no idea where the play might go or what might happen to the characters; the solutions evolved by trial and error, which is fairly standard when a writer confronts blank pages armed with half-formed notions or specifics only of the fuzzier kind. I rewrote the play, or parts of it, perhaps a dozen times before its workshop production at Memphis State University—the first time *Hank Williams* "got on its feet"—and then rewrote again immediately afterwards; changes were also made after a staged reading at Actors Studio in New York. Other changes were subsequently made during, or after, each of the play's first three full productions at New Playwrights' Theatre in Washington, the Live Oak Theatre in Austin and the WPA Theatre in New York. Initial productions of almost any play are more valuable to the playwright for revealing what the play lacks rather than for what it contains. Weaknesses seem to leap out more than strengths.

It became obvious early in the writing that I had returned to basic themes scattered throughout the body of my work: loss and attrition, changes wrought by time, the complexities of generational love, those rough sailings encountered on the seas of romantic love, the manipulative and meddling qualities of people, the difficulties of private communications, and three characteristics indigenous to my original time and place—bullying officialdom, careless violence and barking religious fundamentalism. But I did not realize until I had completed the fifth or sixth rewrite of my play that—at bottom—to a strong degree it dealt with members of my family and my convoluted relationships with them. This now obvious "secret" was first pointed out by my wife, Barbara S. Blaine, who also happens to be my lawyer and literary agent. I rewarded her perspicacity with angry oaths and futile denials. Once I accepted that truth, however, it assisted the shaping of the play's characters and the focusing of events.

Texans who have seen this play have asked exactly where "Stanley, Texas" is located. The best I can say is that it's some forty to sixty miles obliquely west of Odessa in the West Texas badlands where I worked on pipeline crews, as an oil-field roustabout and—briefly—as a roughneck, before seizures of acrophobia brought me down from the rig to the welcoming ground. Stanley is not Monahans, though there are references to the Monahans Sandhills State Park and to an old radar station there (which actually was at long-defunct Pyote Air Force Base *near* Monahans); it could be any of dozens of small towns in the oil patch: Wickett, Mentone, Crane, McCamey, Pyote, Notrees, Wink, you name it—except that I chose not to give Stanley a drop of oil. This was not for reasons of whimsy, but to underline the hopelessness of any community future. But Stanley has, in common with the towns named, a mutual fate of having been bypassed by a new superhighway and left to wither as traffic thundered by "at speeds that don't care what's behind," in the words of the song opening the play. But whatever town Stanley most closely resembles, I was in it—and it will always be in, and with, me.

So I didn't, after all, totally escape.

OF THE VARIED types of writing I have tried—journalism, television documentaries, novels, screenplays, nonfiction books, children's books, song writing—none is as satisfying as writing for the stage.

There is no thrill like seeing a world one has created come alive, night after night, and witnessing the reactions of audiences. Each production of any given play is a new adventure, for good or ill, actors and directors making choices unique unto themselves and the play's look or mood changing according to set design, lighting, sound selections and costuming. Sometimes the author is made proud; sometimes he cringes and bites his tongue. *Nothing* is a certainty; even the individual performances of a given production greatly vary; so, accordingly, do audiences. That element of mystery, of surprise, of the unexpected and the unknown, appeals to me. It is rather like being in a glorious, high-stakes crapshoot with your bankroll and future on the line. It is also hard on the heart and the psyche.

Writing books is a much more solitary exercise; unless the author has the great good luck to visit the best-seller lists or wallow in unusual critical adulation, book writing often seems an exercise in futility. After a short burst of reviews, the comments of one's close friends and a smattering of letters from strangers who care enough to write, a disturbing silence descends. It is like a small death. Something that has long been alive in us and struggling to breathe is suddenly without discernible pulse. Nothing looks quite so dusty and dead as yesterday's book on the shelf; the author likely will begin to brood that the months or years invested in his work have gone for naught. It is at this point that writers become difficult to live with. They may take up with drink, flirt with Godless religions or seek to run with stray blondes. One's worth and how one has chosen to spend one's days are called into question.

Film performances—whether on movie or television screens—are forever frozen and shall never vary for better or worse. A stinking movie (such as, say, *The Best Little Whorehouse in Texas*) can never be fumigated. The stage, by contrast, offers the promise of repeated resurrections and fresh interpretations. New life.

The main problem with writing exclusively for the stage, however, is that productions may be difficult to come by. If it is possible for any one thing to be deader than yesterday's book, that one thing is the unproduced play. Unproduced plays, indeed, are stillborn babies in the minds of their authors. No matter how much the play-wright loves his play or believes in it, his faith has no foundation until proved—or, sadly, disproved—on the stage. So many factors, most of which the writer cannot control, enter into decisions about whether a play will or will not be produced that the playwright is a perpetual candidate for the loony bin.

After the worldwide stage success of *The Best Little Whorehouse in Texas*, I originally assumed that should I write a laundry list producers would line up to wrestle for it. My next outing was a one-man play, based on the life of the late Louisiana politician Huey Long. *The Kingfish* was written as a one-man play to economically show producers its potential worth as a big, money-coining musical. My assumption was that a low-cost one-man showcase production, in which the protagonist talked to and interacted with twenty-three invisible characters, would reveal my material's musical potential. In truth, I had trouble getting producers to look at it—or even to send their representatives. This, perhaps, reflected twin prejudices common to New York producers: (1) that one-man shows aren't lucrative financially and (2) that any stage work accomplished on the wrong side of the George Washington Bridge cannot possibly amount to anything. There is some truth to the former of these be-liefs, and absolutely none in the latter, but there you are. Of those few money men who saw *The Kingfish*, none discovered its mar-velous musical potential even with my shilling guidance. The show ran for three weeks to good notices in Washington in 1979 and then disappeared off the artistic radar screens as if it had crashed and burned, though in 1988 it was revived in New Orleans and toured towns in Louisiana and Texas. My original investment in *The King-fish* was $10,000 for production costs, perhaps another $2,000 for promotional costs and a year in time; to date, it has made a profit of perhaps $3,000 above original costs . . . and can never give back my time. The contrast between the respective fates of *Whorehouse* and *The Kingfish* lends credence to the old playwright's bromide that "you can occasionally get rich in the theater, but it is almost impos-sible to make a living there." Still, I'm not complaining: *The King-fish* at least *has* been produced and enjoys a fitful life a decade after the writing. Of the thousands of plays written each year, relatively few can make even that modest claim. I am a lucky playwright in that five of the six plays I have written to date have gained multiple productions. (I believe the sixth might have, had it not been long bogged in a legal quagmire over who controls the rights; the matter is still unresolved.)

The Night Hank Williams Died was the most difficult of my plays to get onstage. My own misguided enthusiasm helped delay it, although—as we shall see—I had help from others. *My* mistake was in rushing copies to numerous producers before the script was "ripe" and when it contained too many characters to make economic sense. One simply does not submit a play containing fourteen characters, all of whom require salaries, in the absence of a big brassy musical full of special effects, trombones and dancing girls. Unless one's name is Neil Simon, you see, "straight" plays do not as a rule generate enough box-office revenue to support a large cast. Stephanie Phillips, who produced *Whorehouse* for the New York and world stage, perhaps spoke for producers everywhere when she turned down my play with the comment, "Call when you've written another big musical or a one-set, two-person comedy suitable for stars." Producers aren't in the business for reasons of altruism and are rarely blinded by sentiment. The general knock on *Hank Williams* by New York producers was that it didn't appear to be "commercial" enough.

In March of 1985, as I was whittling the cast size and rewriting, a fellow West Texan—Dr. Keith Kennedy, originally of Lamesa—invited me to a production of *Whorehouse* he was directing at Memphis State University where he had long headed the drama department. I must have been invited to five hundred *Whorehouse* openings by then, and normally turned them down for reasons of work, family and frazzlement. But something compelled me to accept Dr. Kennedy's invitation. I liked his production of *Whorehouse* and began to tell him of *Hank Williams;* he saw a rare opportunity for his drama students to observe, and even to participate in, the making of a new play. For the next few weeks I mailed Keith Kennedy each scene as rewrites were completed; his students staged them under his direction, then he and the students sent me their comments and/or suggestions. Some were off the wall; others proved helpful in the developmental process. Dr. Kennedy proposed a workshop production, using professional actors from the Memphis area, for mid-November and I quickly consented.

Meanwhile, some months earlier, I had sent the script and all subsequent rewrites to Peter Masterson, the expatriate Texan actor-director in New York who'd had the original notion to turn my *Playboy* article about a certain Texas "chicken ranch" into a musical comedy and who subsequently had codirected *Whorehouse* with Tommy Tune. Pete liked *Hank*. He arranged a staged reading in October of '85 at the famed Actors Studio in New York, where it was well received. Indeed, Studio officials immediately voted to fund a full showcase production in the upcoming spring. Merry was the playwright: *Whorehouse* had started down happy trails as just such a showcase work at Actors Studio.

Back to Memphis for the workshop production at MSU. I saw a lot I liked and spotted some weaknesses soon repaired by rewrites. Thus Keith Kennedy had given me a valuable production. As a bonus, the Memphis workshop cast Mark Johnson as Thurmond Stottle and he was superb; later I would bring him to Washington to successfully re-create the same role. But that was a long way in the future, and I am getting a big cart before the horse.

About a month after Memphis, Peter Masterson invited me to New York to see the world premiere of his new movie, *A Trip to Bountiful*, which he had directed from Horton Foote's great script. *Bountiful* was a fine, impressive film—critically acclaimed—and in her last movie the late Geraldine Page would win a richly deserved Oscar as the old woman intent on seeing her home in Bountiful, Texas one last time. The next morning, over coffee, Masterson proposed lunch with one of the money men who'd financed *Bountiful*, George Yaneff. "George and I want to produce your play Off-Broadway in the spring," he said, "and then take an option for a movie." Yaneff, during lunch in a swank private club, enthusiastically endorsed the deal. I asked what about the production at Actors Studio? Well, they said, showcase productions are for the purpose of finding producers or investors and here you are with two willing and eager producers sitting before you; in short, I didn't need Actors Studio. That made sense to me. I withdrew *Hank* from the Studio. Soon Masterson and I were examining Off-Broadway houses. Two budgets were drawn up ($350,000 for a 299-seat house; $450,000 for a larger mid-house) and lawyers commenced their ritual quibblings over contractual specifics.

Things went splendidly until the first postponement, indirectly occasioned by the critical success of *A Trip to Bountiful*. The quality of that film caused Masterson to get, and investigate, other movie offers. Though none of them immediately panned out, the talks took time. Opening of *Hank* was pushed back from spring to the fall of '86. Then, in the fall, Masterson said the actor he wanted to play Gus Gilbert would be unavailable until "later." Fall passed, and snow fell. Masterson then said he would be tied up shooting and editing a movie for several months and would require an option giving him until October of 1987 to bring *Hank* Off-Broadway. I said I just wouldn't wait that long and intended to begin shopping the script to others. This inspired Masterson-Yaneff to promise a production by June of 1987. Lawyers resumed their contractual natterings.

By spring of '87 a contract had been drawn to the apparent satisfaction of all parties. The day before I was to fly from my Washington home to New York for the signing—George Yaneff winging in from London for the ceremonies—I discovered over morning coffee a *New York Times* story describing Off-Broadway theater as being in the foulest financial shape in history: the clear inference was that one might make more money raising hogs in Appalachia or stuffing coins in casino slot machines. I had a sudden sinking feeling. It proved not to be misplaced. Peter Masterson soon called to say, Well, uh, too bad but that story in the *Times* had scared everybody witless; they, ah, had concluded, er, this just wasn't the time to invest in an Off-Broadway play. I sat dumbstruck. Masterson made soothing sounds and said maybe a little later he might be interested in taking a movie option on *Hank* for a modest fee. I was not soothed, then or now. My property had been tied up for almost two years and

I had not received a dime, while spending about $6,000 in travel, legal fees and other developmental costs. Such things happen in Show Biz, yes, but that does not mean one has to like it.

I began mailing copies of *Hank* to all New York producers I had marginally encountered and some known to me only as names in the newspapers. Soon a man who had produced plays on both coasts, representing himself as much beloved by theater owners everywhere, expressed enthusiasm for the project. I checked the gentleman out with theatrical sources. They said he was a pest, a liar, a troublemaker, maybe a thief and they would prefer breaking out in hives to doing business with him. Back to the drawing board.

A gregarious, cheerful Southern gentleman entered the game. He talked optimistically big for months before admitting he could pay only $2,000 in front for an option rather than the $5,000 asking price. I deduced that a fellow who couldn't raise five g's might have trouble raising four hundred of them. A third man, charming and well-connected with the respected New York Shakespearian Festival, bought me dinner and said he wanted an option on *Hank*. A contract was being drawn up when Wall Street crashed downward five hundred points in a single day, wiping out at least a half-trillion in national wealth . . . and one would-be producer. At this point I clearly understood that God was punishing me for having impetuously withdrawn my play from the good folks at Actors Studio. I was tempted to reapproach the Studio czars hat in hand, cringing and whining like Uriah Heep, but was paralyzed by pride and fear of rejection.

Well, to hell with New York: it wasn't the only town where theater was practiced. I began sending my script to regional and local theaters throughout the country. The problem with such a scatter-gun approach is that no central clearinghouse exists and, in the absence of personal contacts in such theaters, one's script comes in "over the transom" with hundreds or thousands of look-alikes and, at first glance, bears no distinguishing scars or marks. No theater or theatrical company in America, even if located in a back-alley warehouse or basement, is short of scripts begging to be done. Other than the number of simply terrible plays that get written, here are some reasons accounting for the desperation of playwrights:

(1) More new plays are written than there are resources to stage them; (2) most theaters, facing financial realities, prefer to do proven plays rather than risk the unknown; (3) production costs are ever on the rise; (4) production money is difficult to come by, the vast majority of plays never returning a dime in profits to investors; in the case of nonprofit theaters, grants and gifts have been on the decline for the past decade due, in part, to belt tightening in the arts field by governmental units beset by other problems; (5) it is difficult for playwrights to get their scripts in the hands of the "right" stage director, literary director or selection committee in a timely fashion. They hear, "We *love* your play . . . but, unfortunately, we did another detective story (or domestic comedy or martians-visit-earth yarn) last season"; (6) most theaters aren't staffed with enough readers to wade through all the scripts they receive, so scripts may (a) long gather dust and cobwebs or (b) receive only perfunctory looks from some harassed first reader—often a volunteer or college intern—who may know little more about producible scripts than about brain surgery.

One more shot at New York. I telephoned the office of a Broadway Biggie to say I wanted to send him my script but knew that he—like most Biggies—probably didn't accept unsolicited materials. A nice lady assured me she had loved *Whorehouse,* would be on the look-out for my script, and would see that the Biggie gave it a prompt and careful reading. A week later my script came back marked UNSOLICITED MATERIALS NOT ACCEPTED. I called again and received an apology along with the nice lady's pledge that *everyone* would be alerted to watch for my marvelous script. I remailed it in a fresh envelope adorned by another five dollars worth of virgin stamps. It came flying back freshly stamped UNSOLICITED MATERIALS NOT ACCEPTED. Yes, I called again. The nice lady was no longer employed by The Biggie. Her replacement frostily said Mr. Biggie didn't accept unsolicited materials. . . .

Do not think I had overlooked my native state or my adopted

hometown, Washington, in seeking a production. If theaters in Dallas, Fort Worth, Austin or Houston received my scripts they did not think even to acknowledge them. At a social occasion in Washington I met Peter Sellars, then associated with the Kennedy Center, shortly after the "boy wonder" director had put green laser-beam lights and fog in an indoor scene of a Chekhov play. Mr. Sellars said a mutual friend, an actor, had told him I'd written a simply *marvelous* play, and why hadn't I sent it to him? I had, I said. Six months ago. Mr. Sellars had the grace to blush while stammering that he would soon call me for lunch so we could talk about my marvelous play. I never heard from him again.

A nice fellow wrote a kindly letter from Washington's Arena Stage saying he liked my play, it was "authentic and persuasive," but he feared "the salty characters you have created" were not quite right for Arena's resident company; he did suggest it might be suited to Jon Jory's well-regarded Actors Studio in Louisville. The verdict from Louisville: "This is very funny material, but we produced a show last year that had a similar flavor, so we regret. . . ."

Ford's Theatre didn't even acknowledge receipt of my script with a postcard, though I personally knew the lady who ran it. Perhaps I should have sent her *The Night Abe Lincoln Died*. (Later, after *Hank* attained two productions and was heading for New York—my "Abe Lincoln" crack having appeared in the newspapers—the lady who runs Ford's Theatre looked me up to say, in some distress, that she had never seen my script and a thorough office search had failed to uncover it. As I subsequently heard the same story from four or five other theater managers, I can only say that my faith in the U.S. Mail has been much diminished.)

Barbara S. Blaine is a loving wife, a wonderful mother, a tough lawyer and a nagging agent. There came a time when she suggested that I should not spend the rest of my life trying to get *Hank* on the boards but should move on to other work and new money. I hotly rejoined that *Hank* would be produced, by God, if we had to do it in our backyard. But, I admit, I was thinking of quitting playwriting for the roofing bidness when I read a *Washington Times* story about the new artistic director at New Playwrights' Theatre, one

Peter Frisch, in the late summer of 1987. Mr. Frisch said his mis-
sion would be to produce new plays, not the tried-and-true, and he
was in the market for "the best scripts I can find." I decided to trust
the U.S. Mail one more time. To my astonishment, within the week
Peter Frisch knocked on my door to say he was eager to produce *The
Night Hank Williams Died* as soon as possible. Had we not both
been boys, I might have kissed him.

FROM THE FIRST I had envisioned the actor Henderson Forsythe
as Gus Gilbert. Forsythe had won a Tony as cussing old Sheriff Ed
Earl Dodd in *Whorehouse,* and I had admired his work since seeing
him years earlier in Preston Jones's *The Last Meeting of the Knights
of the White Magnolias* and *The Oldest Living Graduate.* He for-
tunately liked my *Hank* script, had read the part at Actors Studio's
staged reading and had agreed to play it in the aborted Masterson-
Yaneff production. He also consented to do the role at New Playwrights' in Washington. But after all other roles had been cast—and
only forty-eight hours before our rehearsals would begin—a disturbing call came from Forsythe: he was filming a network television series, its shooting schedule had been extended for six weeks
and he was contractually obligated to stick with it. In short, we suddenly had no Gus. Gus is simply the glue that holds *Hank* together.

Peter Frisch and I rushed to New York for hurried, tardy auditions
and called in actors each of us had worked with before. William
Hardy, a displaced Texan who had played in the Houston and second national touring companies of *Whorehouse* as Sheriff Dodd, was
cast in the role—for about six hours. Then he learned he could not
quit a play running in Connecticut on such short notice. We offered
the role to a second Texan and *Whorehouse* veteran, Kevin Cooney.
He accepted. But, again within hours, Cooney recanted on the good
grounds that he simply couldn't afford to work for the small money
available. All other aspirants seemed too "ethnic" or paraded too
many Shakespearian trills or had too much of Brooklyn in their
voices: one simply could not imagine them as crusty old West Texas
barkeeps.

Coming back from New York, Peter Frisch shot me a glum look

and said—over the rattle and clatter of AMTRAK rails—"You're Gus. At least you *sound* right."

Though immediately intrigued by the notion of temporary stardom, I made dutiful sounds of protest.

"No," Frisch said, "you substituted for Forsythe in *Whorehouse* and nobody got killed. So get ready to do it again." It was not, perhaps, the warmest endorsement a director ever gave an actor but I had to be content with it.

I had great fun playing Gus, yes, but working as an actor handicapped me as a playwright. Concerned with my own role, determined not to make an ass of myself under bright lights, I became afflicted by narrow vision. I did not have the luxury of time for reflection or that broad view so necessary to a playwright in the formative production of a new work. Consequently, I permitted one vital scene to be cut—the confrontation between Nellie Bess and her mother. Without that scene the audience merely heard, but did not *see*—a vital difference—how the mother's crazed devotion to religious fundamentalism led her daughter to become tragically manipulative of Thurmond in order to escape Stanley and her mother's clutches. (The "missing scene" was restored for subsequent productions.)

But if emergency casting hurt my play in one way, it accidentally helped it in another. Because we could not find an adequate older Sheriff Royce Landon during auditions, I rewrote the role for a younger man, making him a "Junior" who had recently succeeded to his father's longtime office. This permitted tensions between the young Sheriff and Thurmond—his calendar contemporary—over Nellie Bess, and made more believable the actions to follow. I think it also permitted helpful commentary on the tightly-knit closed society the "courthouse gang" often fashions in small towns, which almost always leads to careless treatment of the powerless. Thus, by a happy accident, my play was enriched by added authenticity.

The Night Hank Williams Died opened at New Playwrights' Theatre, under the able direction of Peter Frisch, on February 2, 1988, and ran there through March 6. It reaped good-to-excellent notices, won Theatre Lobby's Mary Goldwater Award "for contributions to excellence in the theatre in the Washington area" and, subsequently, won the Helen Hayes Award as Outstanding New Play over *M. Butterfly,* the musical *Elmer Gantry, More Than Names* and *The Rivers and Ravines.* Its success helped kill the notion that *Hank Williams* had no commercial appeal: the show sold 94% of capacity and grossed $61,000 in a small, 125-seat house. Still, I did not have to beat off commercial producers with a stick. Fortunately, a Texan—Drew Dennett of Austin—thought he saw commercial possibilities. He assisted a local production directed by Don Toner at Austin's Live Oak Theatre, where—free of acting duties—I was able to tinker with trouble spots in the script during its eight-week run. Dennett then brought the script to the attention of Kyle Renick, resident artistic director of the 128-seat WPA Theatre in the Chelsea district of New York City. WPA has long had a reputation for developing new plays and sending them onward to long life and commercial success, as it has done with *Little Shop of Horrors, Nuts, Key Exchange, Steel Magnolias* and numerous others. I was delighted that that theater was chosen to introduce *Hank* to New York. More revisions were made in the script. Perhaps the biggest was a new, original song opening the show—"A Slow Waltz in Time"—which popped into my head as I gave director Christopher Ashley a quick three-day tour of the wilds of West Texas; the song describes the land and the people in *Hank.* Ashley later said that visit to the barren reefs of the Trans-Pecos territory helped a North Carolina boy— accustomed to water, trees and lush growths—understand my play better. "I saw what the characters were trying to escape," he said. I doubt that comment will please West Texas booster groups, but I have no doubt it is true or that it helped Chris Ashley's direction.

The Night Hank Williams Died opened at the Off-Broadway WPA Theatre on the night of January 24, 1989—still suspect, apparently, as to its commercial possibilities. Several expatriate Texans in Washington, loyal to a fault, flew to New York for the opening—and later confessed they had come to be with me in the event the evening turned into "a wake" due to critical stabs portending a quick closing. But the next day, after reading Mel Gussow's rave review in *The New York Times,* eight commercial producers and five movie outfits made contact inquiring whether we might be open to "deals." *Hank* played to full houses at WPA Theatre through February 26—extending two weeks past its original schedule—and then Drew Dennett moved it to the 347-seat Orpheum Theatre for an open-ended Off-Broadway run beginning March 31, 1989; in May it was nominated as Outstanding New Play by the New York Outer Critics Circle. I found myself onstage as Gus again, for seventeen performances, when our star—Darren McGavin—took leave to work in a television movie. Ultimately, summer stock and amateur rights were sold to the Samuel French Company and a movie sale was made.

If there is an object lesson to playwrights in this tale, perhaps it is simply that one should never give up on a work one believes in. And that a play doesn't have to begin in New York, anymore, to have a life: after Washington and Austin, numerous theaters around the country expressed interest in producing *Hank*. More and more, local nonprofit theaters and regional theaters are starting and developing plays worthy of a stage life—no matter whether they make it to The Big Apple. It's nice when the Gotham lightning strikes, yes, from the standpoint of the playwright's pocketbook and ego and for the good reason that a New York success almost invariably guarantees many subsequent productions elsewhere. But even if New York "doesn't happen" to a play—and it can't, and won't, in most cases—the day is not necessarily lost. Good theater *does* exist "on the wrong side of the George Washington Bridge."

For a playwright there is no reward like knowing that one's baby is alive and breathing on the stage, *any* stage and may—with luck—touch, or even enrich, the lives of theatergoers wherever they are found.

The
Night
Hank
Williams
Died

Cast of Characters

The Night Hank Williams Died is a six-character play requiring four men and two women.

T H U R M O N D S T O T T L E: At age twenty-seven, he is a former high school football hotshot who alternately recalls his old glories and dreams of becoming a country-western singing star and songwriter. In reality, he is a rather ill-equipped fellow who works as a gas-pumper and apprentice mechanic at a service station. He uses alcohol, superimposed on his memories and his daydreams, to lift him above the tedious realities of his day-to-day existence. Left to his own devices, Thurmond would never leave his native place of Stanley, Texas to seek a larger world.

G U S G I L B E R T: Age about sixty. Owner/bartender of the scruffy beer joint with a title much grander than it is: The Sundowner Recreational Club. Gus, like Thurmond, has spent his entire life in Stanley but has lived to regret it. Somewhat cynical and scarred, he has a hidden sentimental streak and is a true good guy at heart. His dangerous quality is that he is willing for others to risk fuller adventures in life than he himself has risked. He has long ago given up on himself but still attempts to play dime-store God to others. He particularly goads Thurmond Stottle to leave town for better opportunities, almost as if Thurmond is expected to live life as a surrogate for Gus. Gus expects no surprises in life and at this stage wants none. He has a strong paternal love for Nellie Bess. Indeed, in his own mind it is quite possible—even likely—that he is her real father.

N E L L I E B E S S P O W E R S C L A R K: Age twenty-six. Thurmond's high school sweetheart and, almost inevitably, head cheerleader to his former football star role. She "broke up" with Thurmond on graduation almost a decade ago, probably because he lacked sufficient ambition and she was determined to move on to better than

3

her hometown provided. She went away to Beauticians College in Abilene, the best fate then available to her, and in fairly short order married a chiropractor whom she would have much preferred to be a medical doctor. Though brighter than most people her life permits her to encounter, Nellie Bess feels dependent on men—not unusual for her time, place, and social station—and threatened or uncertain without one. She is a victim of her culture and misplaced in it. We meet Nellie Bess as her life is in fresh disarray; she is separated from her husband and considering a divorce.

MOON CHILDERS: About fifty-five. Best buddy of Gus and a regular customer. A happy-go-lucky type who likes his beer, playing dominoes, and his undemanding job delivering the products of Aunt Clara's Bakery. Born to small-town life, he is equipped for no other clime by experience or temperament. One of life's easy marks—bad things have a way of happening to Moon—he is able to roll with the punches and sleeps well. Moon will die a great unwashed Nobody when his time comes, but he hasn't thought of that and it wouldn't trouble him much if he should think of it.

SHERIFF ROYCE LANDON, JR.: About thirty-two. A hotshot rookie Sheriff who has succeeded his father in the job; "Old Royce" held the job for twenty-eight years and the younger Sheriff considers the office his by right of birth. Bored by the routine of his small-town job and perhaps seeing himself as the reincarnation of the old frontier western lawman, he goes a long way in trying to drum up business for his jail. Compassion is not in him: it is "Us" against "Them." Gus considers him "armed and dangerous." No love has been lost between Gus and "Old Royce" going back to their schoolboy years, a relationship of acrimony rooted in each of them having courted Vida Powers in bygone years; "Young Royce" is more than happy to carry on this old family feud. The young Sheriff thinks of Thurmond as a worthless bum harboring the potential for big trouble and feels he should be in jail as a matter of principle. And there is a tension between the Sheriff and Thurmond because the former, too, has "sniffed around after Nellie Bess" in the past.

MRS. VIDA POWERS: About fifty. She is the mother of Nellie Bess and a certified religious nut. Long a widow. She claims Jesus calls on her personally, perhaps to discuss Baptist theology and the shortcomings of all other mortals residing in Stanley, Texas. Has raised her only child "in the Kingdom of the Lord" and is bitterly disappointed that Nellie Bess has not lived up to saintly expectations. Not one humorous bone in this woman's body: her Jesus is the angry one who chased the money changers from the temple and turned Lot's wife into a pillar of salt, not the kindly young Jehovah who fed multitudes by miracles of loaves and fishes or forgave harlots and thieves. She sees life as a testing, a fight against temptation; anything of fun or pleasure means you've failed the test. She is perhaps overcompensating for having known a few loose pleasures as a young woman, before religion came to her harsh rescue. Faith may have made *her* daily life bearable, but in whipping others with it she has spread misery enough for a small army.

Sets and Locations

The action occurs in roughly a six-week span in the summer of 1952. Ike is on the way to becoming President and Harry Truman is winding down his term. The Korean War is in full flower. It is a summer of hot weather and a prolonged drought.

The 1950 Census found 2,378 people in Stanley, Texas—not all of them happily located. Each year a few more die or move away and rarely are they replaced. Stanley has nowhere to go but up, but—alas—will never again move in that direction. Carlton County has the dubious distinction of being the only county in the huge Permian Basin oil pool where God and/or nature failed to provide a drop of the profitable, underground "dinosaur wine." Oil abounds on all sides of oil-less Carlton County, making the lack of this rich blessing harder to take for most of the locals.

Times are consequently rough in this desert outpost. Ranching is the economic hope of the town, but the drought has crippled cattlemen. Business is slow. Greyhound Lines discontinued daily bus service several years ago, and even the Chamber of Commerce—with little to cheer—has disbanded.

The main set is the interior of the Sundowner Recreational Club.

Downstairs is the main barroom. Upstairs is suggested a simple room where Gus Gilbert, the owner/bartender, lives a spartan life. Stairs running down from that room to behind the bar permit Gus to come and go from "work" to "home."

The downstairs barroom is equipped with six barstools at the bar and two or three small tables. A lift-up panel at each end of the bar permits Gus to have easy access to the barroom itself. Beer signs are posted: Jax, Pearl, Pabst Blue Ribbon, Texas Morning Dew. None of

7

the beer signs should look new. No liquor bottles are displayed behind the bar: Texas in the 1950s permitted no "mixed" drinks or hard liquor to be sold except in private clubs licensed as such. The Sundowner Recreational Club—despite its name—is far from that; there is a domino table and a pool table—either onstage or suggested in a rear "poolroom." (If no pool table is used, the domino table becomes Gus's "sacred" possession.) Otherwise, a jukebox is the only "recreational facility."

Behind the bar is a big corkboard, a catch-all community bulletin board. Thumbtacked to it are old, curling notices both typed and handwritten. Three postings should be large enough to be readable: (1) A homemade sign, running uphill and down as if perhaps painted in the dark, announcing "ABSOLUTELY NO BEER TABS TO NOBODY." (2) A purple-and-gold bumper sticker imploring "GO JACKRABBITS GO!" (3) A sign advertising "SWEETWATER RATTLESNAKE ROUNDUP" to be held on July 4, 1948, and announcing an Entry Fee of $5.00. A framed photograph of a small football squad is prominent as the corkboard's centerpiece.

Centered behind the bar, on the wall in the cradling rack, is an operable pump-action shotgun.

A black telephone of the 1950s period hangs from the wall behind the bar, near the steps leading up to the small room where Gus lives. Behind the bar on a shelf or table is a radio of the 1950s era. Somewhere is a poster, with picture, reading "Re-Elect Sheriff Royce Landon, Jr."

One small, simple set other than the bar set is used during Act Two, though it is more "suggested" than not. It suggests the interior of a car at a drive-in theater; a cutaway view, seen head on, as if looking inside the car from in front of the hood. The two characters playing the scene, Thurmond and Nellie Bess, will face the audience while ostensibly watching a movie on a big outdoor screen. A car speaker will be needed to run from the mobile speaker stand beside the car,

into the driver's side. The effect of a car at a drive-in movie may be heightened by darkness on the stage around the car, and the car itself should be in a single spotlight. You will need a sound track of a war movie for sounds of battle: guns, airplanes, and so on.

The theater audience on arrival will see the barroom set. Suggest bright and lively country music to warm up the crowd before the curtain, though *not* any of the tunes to be used in the play proper.

into the driver's side. The effect of a car at a drive-in movie may be heightened by darkness on the stage around the car, and the car itself should be in a single spotlight. You will need a sound track of a war movie for sounds of battle: guns, airplanes, and so on.

The theater audience on arrival will see the barroom set. Suggest bright and lively country music to warm up the crowd before the curtain, though *not* any of the tunes to be used in the play proper.

Act I / Scene 1

As houselights go dark, so does the stage. We hear, VOICE OVER, *the song "A Slow Waltz in Time." Stage lights slowly come up. We see the interior of the Sundowner Recreational Club; the time is about noon or a bit after. No actor is visible on the stage for a few moments as the song is heard.*

VOICE OVER (*as from jukebox, recorded by actor playing* THURMOND STOTTLE):

> The wind blows high lonesome
> The last horseman's passed by
> Old rivers are powder
> And the sun boils the sky.
> The town's tamed and hobbled
> Making life a sad song
> Where all but old memories
> Have packed up and gone . . .

(THURMOND *appears outside the bar, looking into it from the main window.*)

> Nothing moves on the highway
> That ain't going away
> At speeds that don't care what's behind.
> Tomorrow seems risky
> Too much of a mystery
> And yesterday is a lost friend
> The future can't find . . .

(THURMOND *enters, dressed in faded western garb: cowboy-style summer straw hat with coiled brim, faded and tattered*

blue jeans, work shirt with sleeves rolled up. He carries a bat-
tered guitar.)

> It was a summer like others
> A slow waltz in time
> And given his druthers
> He might move on down the line.
> But cuttin' loose ain't easy
> When you hide in your mind . . .
> Dreamin' deuces are aces
> When your poetry won't rhyme . . .

(T H U R M O N D *seems a bit jumpy and in need of something.)*

T H U R M O N D *(calling lightly):* Gus? Anybody home? *(A beat.)*
Gus? *(Satisfied he is alone, he hurries behind the bar and tugs on
the beer cooler. It is locked.)* Shit!

*(He spots a near-empty beer bottle on the bar and quickly
drinks the warm dregs. He makes a sour face. Once again, he
tugs on the locked beer cooler without success.)*

T H U R M O N D *(coming from behind the bar):* Damned old stingy
gut!

*(He hooks, with a booted foot, one of the cane-bottomed chairs
from near the domino table, sits in it and starts picking out a
ragged tune of his own composition as he sings a snatch of it.)*

> Just gimme
> A little bitty
> Bit of love . . .

*(But he can't get it right. He frowns, runs the guitar riff again
and tries to sing a new variation.)*

Just gimme
A little bitty
Bit of yore luh-huv . . .

(*Still not right. He shakes his head, bites his lip, and attempts yet another version.*)

Just ah-gimme
Uh little ol' bitty
Bit of luh-huh-huv . . .

(*That's the sorriest version yet.* THURMOND *strikes his guitar strings one hard, angry discordant blow and then places his guitar on the pool table. He then wanders to the jukebox to study the selections. As he positions himself,* GUS—*unseen by* THURMOND—*enters from the restroom where the "His" side of the card is showing;* GUS *is zipping up under his soiled apron; a large number of keys are attached to his belt by a long chain.* GUS *pauses to flip the sign on the restroom from "His" to the side reading "Hers" and then glances over at* THURMOND. *But* THURMOND, *still studying the jukebox offerings, is not aware of him.*)

GUS (*crossing to bar*): How many times I told you not to scar my pool table with your friggin' headache box, Thurmond?

(THURMOND *visibly starts, then leaps guiltily to remove the offending guitar. He turns as if to apologize.*)

GUS: And don't go tellin' me how sorry you are. I already know that. You too damn sorry to be blackmailed. Not a damn one of you Stottle Boys could be sold for dog food.

THURMOND: Come on, Gus! Don't be low-ratin' my people.

GUS: That'd be might-nigh impossible.

THURMOND: Now just what in hail have I did to curl your tail? I spent nearly six dollars in this sumbitch last night.

GUS: Don't hand me no six-dollar bullshit! You bought yourself three beers and Billy Gaskins two more, which don't come to but a buck-six-bits. Rest of the time, y'all mooched off that drunk fly-boy from the Monahans Radar Station.

THURMOND: But I spent the rest shootin' pool! Money all goes in the same pocket, don't it?

GUS: Why they got a damn Radar Station over at Monahans anyway? What the shit's around here worth protectin'?

THURMOND: The guviment's probably worried about your pool table.

(THURMOND *hugely enjoys his joke.* GUS *throws him a hard look, then takes his money box and a ledger from beneath the bar; he begins counting money and jotting sums.* THURMOND *begins idly strumming his guitar.*)

THURMOND: How long you owned this ol' place, Gus?

GUS: Too long. You wadn't even a gleam in your daddy's eye.

THURMOND: You'd prob'ly make more money if you'd open this broke-down ol' joint before one-damn-thirty. And a man could get a beer when he needed it.

GUS: A man would need money. And maybe I don't want no damnyankee tourist comin' in orderin' me to cook him a lunch of pizza-and-bagels.

THURMOND: *Tourist?* I ain't seen a tourist since they opened the new By-Pass! And that was back before the War started.

G U S: It ain't a *war,* it's a "Po-leece Action." Don't you listen to what President Truman says?

T H U R M O N D: I don't listen to no politician. It was the goddamn politicians that let 'em curve that road around this town and leave us to rot on the vine.

G U S: Why you give a damn? Last night you was hell-bent on goin' off to Nashville to become the new Roy Acuff.

T H U R M O N D: Roy Acuff's hind laig! I'm more in the style of Hank Williams.

G U S: Funny I hadn't heard nobody else mention that.

(T H U R M O N D *gives his guitar an angry whack and jumps to his feet.*)

T H U R M O N D: Why don't you let up on me? There's lotsa sum-bitches come in here sorrier than I am!

G U S: Name one.

T H U R M O N D: Well . . . damn you, Gus!

G U S: I stay on your butt, Hero, hopin' to persuade you to sickle on outta this dried-up cactus patch before you wither plumb away. You don't hafta be Hank Williams to better yourself! Git off your rusty-dusty and find yourself a roughneckin' job! Hell, boy, the drillin' rigs is workin' twenty-four hours over around Odessa and Midland.

T H U R M O N D: I . . . cain't do that.

G U S: Why, you paralyzed?

THURMOND (*embarrassed*): Them oil rigs is too high, Gus. I'm scared a them tall thangs.

GUS (*irritated*): Then go to West Virginia and work in a goddamn coal mine! (*A beat.*) Damn if you ain't got more excuses than a drinkin' preacher.

THURMOND: There's my band, Gus. I cain't just up and run off and desert my goddamn *band*.

GUS: Some band! Last job that bunch played was the Freshman dance, four years ago. Now them kids is Seniors and knows too much about music to hire "Thurmond Stottle" and his . . . "Trottin' Turkeys," or whatever you call 'em.

THURMOND: It's the "Stompin' Cowpokes" and you damn well know it!

GUS (*chuckling*): Ain't that pitiful? Can't none of you ride a damn *horse*.

THURMOND: What's that got to do with the price of rice? The "Stompin' Cowpokes" is just a *name*. Like . . . well, like the "Brooklyn Dodgers" or . . . the "Stanley High Jackrabbits"!

GUS (*grinning, as he swabs the bar*): Yeah, I guess them big music mo-guls in Nashville can't hardly wait to git their hands on a big new country singin' star by the outstandin' name of "Thurmond Stottle."

THURMOND: You ever heard of Lester Flatt? Hawkshaw Hawkins? (*Consulting jukebox for more names.*) Uh, Moon Mullican? T. Texas Tyler? And how about Homer and Jethro, huh? Listen, you old fart, Homer and Jethro made more money last year playin' the Odessa Oil Show in *three days* than this crappy ol' beer joint would take in in a month of goddamn Sundays!

GUS: The difference between you and them other fellers with peculiar names, "Thurmond," is that *they* learned to play their fuckin' guitars.

THURMOND (*disgusted*): Aw . . . blow it out your ditty bag!

(THURMOND *stalks to the jukebox and searches himself for coins, but finds none. He then turns back to* GUS. *Wheedling.*)

Hey, Gus, how about trippin' the jukebox?

GUS: You trip it. I ain't mad at it.

(*He much enjoys his joke.*)

THURMOND: I ain't got a dime, Gus! If they was givin' away free tumbleweeds, I couldn't afford the wind to get mine home.

GUS: I thought between pumpin' gas for Tood Brandon, and frontin' that hotshot band, you was makin' more money than Homer *and* Jethro.

THURMOND: Money's your God, ain't it? You rate money ahead of women or cars or . . . or just about anythang!

GUS: I find it comes in handy if a man takes a notion to play the jukebox.

THURMOND: Awright, awright!

GUS: You won't ever have two nickels to rub together long as you stay buried in this scabby town. And for what? Hangin' on to your mama's tit? Gettin' drunk and yarnin' about your "glory days" as a . . . pimple-faced schoolboy fullback?

THURMOND: Halfback, dammit, *half*back! (*A beat; calmer.*) And there's more to it than you say. This is my *place*, Gus. Ever' memory I got in my head, just about, is tied to this ol' town.

G U S: Them memories and a dime will buy you a cuppa coffee.

T H U R M O N D: My *roots* is here, Gus! Why, hail, the Indian Wars was barely over when the first Stottles settled in this parta the country! And they stayed on to farm and run cattle . . . and . . . they *owned* thangs. This land *meant* somethin' to 'em, by God, and when they died they give their bones to it. And I . . . well, hail, I just cain't hardly turn my back on all that. It weighs on me!

G U S (*disbelieving*): God-a-mighty, Boy, you've seen way too many cowboy movies. Your people wadn't land barons or cattle kings, they was a buncha sharecroppers and oil-field trash! And as for the damned *land,* it wore out about fifty years ago. (*Grumbling.*) Kiss my foot, a boy that can't hardly read and write tells me he's weighed down by goddamned *history!*

T H U R M O N D: Well even if I had the money to go somewheres and start over—which I don't—how do I know I'd like it?

G U S (*exasperated*): Well how you know you *won't?*

T H U R M O N D (*hesitant; a bit shamed*): I . . . learnt in the Navy I don't take to strangers good. I have trouble talkin' to people that's . . . different. Or that's got habits I don't unnerstand.

G U S (*disgusted; giving up*): Well maybe the guviment oughta give some perfesser a goddamn . . . *grant* to study a boy as peculiar as you!

(G U S *turns away and goes behind the bar.*)

T H U R M O N D (*after a beat*): How about a beer, Gus?

GUS: You know my house rules. No beer tabs for nobody.

THURMOND (*quietly*): I need it, Gus.

GUS: What you *need* is a kick in your lazy butt.

THURMOND (*shouting*): *I need it, Gus! Fuck your chicken-shit rules!*

(*He pounds the bar;* GUS *stares at him, astonished, then quickly fishes out a beer, opens it, and places it on the bar.* THURMOND *grabs it and drinks as if feverish, in huge gulps; he breaks for air.*)

GUS (*concerned; mildly*): Son . . . that kinda drinkin's likely to damage what's left of your brain.

(THURMOND *finishes killing the beer in long, desperate gulps, as if receiving an emergency transfusion. He stands a moment, breathing hard, then takes a couple of steps toward the bar—holding the empty bottle—as if making a silent, desperate request for one more beer.* GUS, *watching him, almost imperceptibly shakes his head and makes a humanitarian decision.*)

GUS: What the hell: in for a nickel . . . in for a dime.

(*He opens another beer and pushes it across the bar.* THURMOND *seizes it eagerly, though this time his first gulp is more controlled.* GUS *takes a pad and begins writing out the tab.*)

GUS: Now don't forget that'll be seventy cents you owe me come Friday. And *don't* go runnin' your mouth I put you on a tab. Ain't nothin' *in* this fly-blown village but deadbeats and a few crazy preachers.

(*He thrusts the pad toward* THURMOND.)

Put your John Hancock on there.

THURMOND: Just keep a runnin' tab, Gus, 'til I'm through.

GUS: Bullshiiiiit!

  (*He snatches away* THURMOND*'s beer;* THURMOND *grabs the pad and scrawls his name, then* GUS *presents him the beer in mock fashion.*)

GUS (*folding tab; putting it in billfold*): You seen Nellie Bess since she got back?

THURMOND: No, by God. There's a old song that's already been sung.

GUS: Ah, Nellie Bess is a good kid. At least *she* had gumption enough to *adios* her old hometown quick as she could raise a bus ticket.

THURMOND (*derisively*): You think she's any better off down in Cisco?

GUS: She'd be better off in a Meskin jail than in this snakepit.

  (*He takes his breakfast from under the counter—two beers and a chocolate donut—and crosses to a table.*)

THURMOND: Well thanks a whole damn bunch! I guess you've forgot whose damned engagement rang she give back when she quit town.

GUS: Yeah . . . that musta broke poor ol' Abe Zale's heart.

THURMOND: Dammit, Gus, it was *me* she give the rang back to.

G U S (*enjoying it*): But Abe was the one carryin' the bank paper on it.

T H U R M O N D: Oh that's real funny!

(G U S *laughs.*)

Nellie Bess ain't done so damn hot, if you're askin' me. What's so uptown about marryin' a Cisco chiropractor?

G U S: Yeah, poor girl. She could of stayed here and married a gas pumper and become real big in the Junior League.

(T H U R M O N D *snorts and takes another beer hit;* G U S *begins eating breakfast.*)

T H U R M O N D (*relaxing; reflecting*): Aw, we had us some good ol' times, me and Nellie Bess. Never will forget that Senior Trip to El Paso. Me and her set in the back of that ol' school bus and swapped spit from the city limits on!

G U S: Sorry I missed it, romantic as you make it sound.

T H U R M O N D: Out there around Van Horn, when we stopped to stretch at a roadside park? Well, by God, we got officially engaged! I give her a King Edward cigar band for a rang.

G U S: Didja rent her a lock box?

T H U R M O N D: Dammit, that cigar band was just temporary! (*A beat.*) Anyhow, when we got to El Paso us football boys scooted across the border to War-As. To check out them little *senoritas* at places like Erma's House-of-All-Nations and Mexicali Rose's? Wow! You talk about your hot pepper on the hoof! (*Laughs.*) We . . . we come rollin' back to that El Paso ho-tel near-bout daylight, bombed outta our gourds and smellin' a little bit like stray wimmen. Wellsir, Nellie Bess was waitin' up in that ho-tel lobby, pattin' her foot and cryin' and madder'n some old wet hen.

(Laughs again. Then becomes serious.)

You know, I never have unnerstood why she threw me over and run off to the damn Beauticians College.

GUS *(dryly)*: Women's sure hard to figger, alright.

THURMOND *(brightening)*: Hollywood didn't have nothin' to touch her, and I don't give a shit if you're talkin' Veronica Lake or Hedy Lamarr! She was all blonde and pink . . . and sometimes kind of a gold tan from the sun. She . . . she kinda *sparkled*, Gus. She kinda . . . shined.

(During this GUS starts to drink the second beer, and then—on impulse—he pushes the beer in front of THURMOND. THURMOND is so lost in reverie he takes a hit from the new bottle without noticing the gift.)

Back in '44 she got elected head cheerleader. I can still see her struttin' in front of that Jackrabbit band! I had a private name for her . . . Miss Sparkles and her Magic Pom-Poms. *If* you get whatta mean?

GUS: 'Fraid I do, yeah.

(THURMOND drinks beer again.)

THURMOND *(happily)*: Boy, if I could freeze *time* I guess I'd ice me down a bucket of 19-and-44! We won the District 5-B Football Championship that year. Won it *walkin'*, by God! Stomped the snot outta the Marfa Shorthorns and the Alpine Bucks and ever-body else. And in the title game, against the Fort Stockton Panthers, I gained a hunnert-and-fifty-six yards from scrimmage and scored three touchdowns! One of 'em—

THURMOND and GUS *(in unison)*: —by God, on a forty-nine-yard punt return!

THURMOND *(surprised and delighted)*: By God, Gus, you still recollect that?

GUS *(rising; impatient)*: Jesus Christ, Thurmond, you give that old football-hero spiel to that drunk fly-boy in here five or six times just last night! Everybody in town's got your bullshit memorized.

(GUS *crosses toward the bar.)*

THURMOND: Lemme see the picture, Gus.

GUS: Here we go wearin' out memory lane again.

(But he takes down the framed photo of the football squad from behind the bar, and throws it on the counter.)

THURMOND *(studying picture)*: That's me, right there in the front row. Old Number Twenty-One. Lookin' mad, bad, and too purty to be had!

GUS: You was just eighteen years old then, Thurmond. Not twenty-seven and workin' on a beer gut.

THURMOND *(serious)*: You know, by God, if I hadn't of chumped off and joined the damn Navy—if I'd went to Texas Tech or Hardin-Simmons like people wanted me to—I might of ended up a All-American! Goddamn right! Mighta had my picture printed on the cover of the *Saturday Evenin' Post* or *Life* or *Collier's*.

GUS: All-American, huh?

THURMOND: Why the hell *not* All-American? I was fast, I could catch the ball, and I was willin' to pay the price!

GUS: You play ball in the Navy?

THURMOND: Damn sure did!

GUS: Then how come you never made All-Navy?

(THURMOND *flings the photo on the bar and turns away;* GUS *picks up the photo.*)

There's nothin' wrong with dreams, Boy. Providin' you act on 'em. But *day*-dreamin', now—shit, that's just buildin' worthless air castles. Fact is, you never had a shot at bein' All-American . . . and you ain't ever gonna be Hank Williams. If you'd admit that much to yourself you could move on to better'n you got.

(*He rehangs the photo;* THURMOND *angles his beer bottle at* GUS, *pointing it like a gun.*)

THURMOND: If you're such a goddamn world-beatin' go-getter, what're you doin' stuck in a broke-down beer joint in a town you talk about like it was a pile a dog turds?

GUS (*quietly*): Well, Son, if you're lucky . . . and look ahead . . . won't nobody ever ask you a question like that.

(*This quiet truth is disconcerting to* THURMOND; *he momentarily is speechless. He rises from his chair, shuffling awkwardly.*)

THURMOND: Well . . . hail. Goddamn. (*A beat.*) I cain't . . . I cain't hang around listenin' to some ol' crazy man runnin' his mouth all day. I got to git to work.

G U S: Don't forget to put on them cute trick britches Tood Brandon makes you wear.

(T H U R M O N D *quickly drains his beer bottle, starts to place it on the bar, and then walks over to smack it down hard and defiantly on the sacred pool table. He stares at* G U S *as if to challenge him*— G U S *returning the hard look*—*then grabs his guitar and scoots out to the street without another word.* G U S *waits until he leaves, shakes his head and comes out from behind the bar to remove the offending bottle from the pool table. He inspects for damages, finds none, shakes his head and crosses toward the bar with the empty beer bottle at . . .*)

B L A C K O U T

(*. . . when a country-western tune
is heard in the dark.*)

Act I/Scene 2

The next day, noonish. While still in blackout, we hear the begin-
ning chatter of a folksy RADIO ANNOUNCER (VO).

RADIO ANNOUNCER (VO): Yessir, Good Neighbors, this is
K-E-R-B, Kermit, the friendly spot on your dial at 920 kilocycles,
and it's exactly 12:42 P.M. give or take a freckle and a hair. The
noon temperature at Winkler County Airport, right here in good
old Kerb Kountry, was ninety-six degrees and climbing . . .

> *(Stage lights come up. We see* GUS *behind the bar, in a different*
> *shirt and the same old dirty apron. He drops two Alka-Seltzer*
> *tablets into a glass of beer, lets it fizz briefly and drinks it. He*
> *makes a horrible face and loudly burps. Meanwhile, the* RADIO
> ANNOUNCER *has continued nonstop.)*

. . . and the mercury's due to reach three digits about three o'clock.
If you're out there waiting for rain, Neighbors, maybe you oughta
pray harder. This is the seventy-third straight day in these parts
without a drop of moisture and I'm telling ya, this doggone old dry
spell has our ranchers and farmers talking to theirselves. But out
here in West Texas, as you Good Neighbors know, all things are
possible and the big, high sky is the limit.

GUS: Horseshit!

RADIO ANNOUNCER (VO): So keep your slickers handy, pard-
ners, just in case those late-afternoon thunderclouds mean business this time.

> *(*GUS *snaps off the radio.)*

GUS: I'll rush out and build a goddamn ark.

(He goes to the domino table and unstacks a chair. He crosses to behind the bar, still cleaning up debris. NELLIE BESS POWERS CLARK enters, hesitating just inside the door long enough for the audience to spot her. She is twenty-six, blonde and attractive, though the bloom has faded a bit from the high school knockout THURMOND has recalled. She wears pedal pushers, a blouse tied to show a bit of bare midriff, sandals, and sunshades; her lips, fingernails, and toenails are painted blood red. As she enters, she pushes her sunshades up on her head and wears them like a crown. After her initial hesitation, she crosses toward the bar.)

NELLIE BESS *(singing it out)*: Hidy, you old sweetheart! Who's your best girl?

GUS *(turning)*: Well Great God from Gal-veston, Nellie Bess, come in this house!

(NELLIE BESS rushes to the bar and they enthusiastically embrace across it.)

NELLIE BESS *(in embrace)*: How you doin', Darlin'?

GUS: Some better, now that you're here! Have a seat, Sugar!

(NELLIE BESS sits on a barstool; GUS beams at her.)

Heard you was in town, and been wonderin' when you was gonna pay me a call.

NELLIE BESS *(with a laugh)*: I've been *trying* to get away from Mama for three days!

GUS: Pop you a cold 'un, Nellie Bess?

NELLIE BESS (*hesitates*): I . . . really ought to content myself with a Coca-Cola.

GUS: I imagine you could of got a Co-Cola at your mama's house.

NELLIE BESS: Well . . . I guess a Pearl wouldn't bite me.

(GUS *produces the beer, opens it, and pushes it across the bar; he beams at* NELLIE BESS *as she takes a healthy pull.*)

NELLIE BESS: Lord, I'd forgotten how hot it can get here in Stanley. Like one big ol' steam bath. And you *know* my mama don't believe in air conditioning, because it's not mentioned in the Bible?

GUS (*smiling*): How is Miz Powers?

NELLIE BESS: Oh, she's still staying in real close touch with Jesus. She saw him again Thursday night. That makes three times this month.

GUS: I don't reckon he let it slip when it might rain?

NELLIE BESS: No, he was too busy covering the finer points of Baptist theology!

(*They chuckle.*)

GUS: Well, Hunnybunch, you lookin' as sound as hard money.

NELLIE BESS: Shoot! I feel like something the cat dragged up and the dogs wouldn't eat, in this ol' heat.

(*She turns on her barstool and inspects the room.*)

Things look pretty much the same around here.

G U S: Discouragin' ain't it?

N E L L I E   B E S S: Anybody much . . . around town this summer?

G U S (*giving her a look*): Oh yeah. He was in here just yesterday about this time.

> (N E L L I E   B E S S, *embarrassed at being so obvious, hides in her beer.*)

Don't tell me you're still carryin' a certain old torch?

N E L L I E   B E S S: Gus! Don't you forget I'm a married woman! (*A beat.*) Or I was the last I heard.

G U S (*quietly*): Honeymoon over, is it?

N E L L I E   B E S S: Don't be talking that around, Gus! Please! I just came home to . . . think a few things out.

G U S: Feel like talkin' about it?

N E L L I E   B E S S: I do . . . and I don't.

G U S: Beer and ketchup was meant to be bottled up. But I don't think things that bothers people was.

N E L L I E   B E S S (*after a beat*): I admit that one day I think . . . I want a divorce. And the next day I'm afraid of it. Maybe if I'd had more education or training . . . (*A beat.*) But *if* frogs had wings they wouldn't bump their fannies when they jump.

G U S (*chuckling*): Yeah, yeah.

N E L L I E   B E S S: What happens to people when they marry, Gus? Why does it go . . . flat?

GUS: I always thought marriage tries to make one person outta two. And sometimes it's hard to git the graft to take.

NELLIE BESS: That why you never took the fatal step?

GUS: Aw, well now, that's . . . that's a long story it's kinda pointless to tell. I'd druther hear yours.

NELLIE BESS: I just can't figure Howard out. He gripes that I spend too much money, but he won't let me work. I don't know what he wants. He seems to prefer eating with the Lions and the Jaycees to eating with me. So I play bridge with "the girls" until I think I'll turn to celery and cheese dip.

GUS: I'm mighty sorry to hear it.

NELLIE BESS: Sometimes I wonder what I could have *seen* in that man!

GUS: Darlin', at age eighteen I imagine you seen whatever you wanted to see.

NELLIE BESS: I'll kiss a fool if *that's* not right! He was young, he had money in his pocket and dreams in his head. And I was a . . . silly little butterfly looking for a flower. I guess, looking back, I saw him as somebody who could take me away from a life of dime-store dishes and dirty work shirts.

GUS: Under them conditions I mighta married the boy myself!

NELLIE BESS: *For sure* I didn't wanta end up like my mama. Fighting over bills and debts with a husband whose job interfered with his drinking. And seeing Jesus jump out from behind every bush. (*A beat.*) I've tried to remember if I truly *loved* Howard back then. All I can really recall is that he drove a good car and could make me laugh. (*A beat.*) And he didn't have a pot belly or warts on his nose so, what the hell, Nellie Bess—say hello to Prince Charming.

(*They laugh; she takes another beer hit.*)

When I was . . . Little Miss Innocent . . . I thought my parents were the only unhappy people in the world. Now I wonder if anybody's truly happy.

GUS: The trouble with most people is they don't know what their lives is all about. And the problem with the *others* is they've discovered their lives ain't about anything much.

NELLIE BESS (*after a beat*): Gus . . . how is he?

GUS: Aw, he's down with a bad case of the Do-Nothings and Don't-Cares. I tell him to move on down the road before he wakes up to discover he's shavin' a forty-year-old man. But, you know Thurmond.

NELLIE BESS: Yes. Or I once did.

GUS: Hell, he ain't changed. Still hopin' when he wakes up it'll be yesterday again.

NELLIE BESS: He never wanted much. Which was the main fault I found with him. I wanted to see the big world and he wanted his own body-and-fender shop in this little old town. And to go to a rodeo occasionally. Play his guitar. Drink some beer.

GUS: Well he's gettin' his share of the beer. And evertime he gets a snootful he dreams about Nashville callin' him to be a big star. But I don't believe the son-of-a-buck would go if they mailed him a first-class ticket.

NELLIE BESS (*smiling*): Not unless it was round-trip.

GUS: You ever think about settlin' down here in Snoozeville yourself?

NELLIE BESS: God forbid! (*Laughs.*) Oh, it *has* crossed my mind occasionally. I forget how ugly this country is when I'm gone. Then I come back and it hits me fresh how flat and brown and bald it looks . . . like some old man that won't take enough baths. And lonesome? My Lord! Nothing to do but listen to the wind howl, or drive around dodging tumbleweeds and orphan dogs. (*Laughs.*) Oh, but Gus, what would the Chamber of Commerce think to hear me talking like that?

GUS: Nothin'. It closed down five years ago.

NELLIE BESS: Do you ever wonder how come we're the *only* county in West Texas without any oil? I mean who, or what, so arranged things that oil pooled up all *around* us and we didn't get a blessed drop?

GUS: I imagine God figured he'd give us so many sand dunes and jackrabbits and Meskins we didn't need nothin' else.

NELLIE BESS (*laughing*): Be serious! I mean, truly, it's almost like there was some . . . higher conspiracy. Some . . . freak plot of nature.

GUS: Aw, some Midland geologist stopped in here a while back and tried to explain it. Talked about "tight sand" and "bad gravity" and the wrong kind of "substructural rock" or some such. He was so overeducated I couldn't hardly follow him.

NELLIE BESS: But it's not *fair*, is it?

GUS: I'm 'fraid the world ain't geared for fair, Nellie Bess.

NELLIE BESS: But think how different our lives might have been! Why, I might have wound up a sorority girl at SMU and married Doak Walker or a Dallas banker!

GUS: Oil ain't always a blessin'. Midland and Houston would of got richer. But about all the common herd would of got is a rough element comin' into the community and prices jumpin' up higher'n a cat's back. Oil, I dunno, somehow it's got a way of makin' people and places greedy and mean.

(NELLIE BESS *jumps off her barstool, claps her hands, and assumes her old cheerleader pose.*)

NELLIE BESS:

> Gimme a G
> Gimme a R
> Gimme a E
> Gimme a E
> Gimme a D
> Yeeeeeeeeeaaaaa, *Greed!*

(*She jumps in the air on her last word; they laugh.*)

GUS: Well I admit I might change my mind if I got cut in on the pie!

NELLIE BESS (*checking her watch*): I guess I'd better run along before Mama sends out a search party. You know how one-way that woman is about drinking!

(*She produces a dollar from her pocket.*)

GUS (*waving her off*): On the house, Nellie Bess.

(THURMOND STOTTLE *rushes in, excited; he wears a billed*

cap and matching coveralls lettered "BRANDON'S ONE-STOP SERVICE.")

THURMOND: Say, Gus, did you hear—

(He stops dead on spotting NELLIE BESS. They stand face-to-face and stare at each other. A long beat.)

GUS: Y'all want me to innerduce ya?

THURMOND: I'll just be goddamned! Nellie Bess Powers herownself!

NELLIE BESS *(nervously)*: It's . . . Nellie Bess Clark, now.

THURMOND: Yeah, well, whatever it is you're a sight for sore eyes. *(A beat.)* Aw, hail, looks like I could of thought of somethin' more original. *(Laughs.)* Can I buy you a brew?

GUS: Now *that's* real original.

NELLIE BESS: Actually, I was just leaving to—

THURMOND: Aw, come on! For old time's sake!

NELLIE BESS: Well . . . maybe just one.

THURMOND: Now you're talkin'!

(They approach the barstools, suddenly awkward with each other. She sits first, after THURMOND almost does but remembers his manners just in time. THURMOND then scrambles onto an adjoining stool.)

THURMOND: Uh, Gus . . .

GUS (*quickly*): On your tab, Thurmond?

THURMOND (*vastly relieved*): Oh, yeah, sure. *Sure!* Same old Gus, Nellie Bess. Says nobody cain't sign tabs and then forces tabs on everbody! I was tryin' to pay cash money just yesterday but he wouldn't hear it. Ain't that right, Gus?

GUS: That's about as close to the truth as you'll ever come.

(GUS *serves their beers;* THURMOND *holds his beer up to propose a toast; he and* NELLIE BESS *clink bottles. They drink, then smile at each other. A long beat during these inspections.*)

THURMOND and NELLIE BESS (*in unison*): Well . . .

(*They laugh self-consciously.*)

THURMOND: Go ahead.

NELLIE BESS: No, you.

THURMOND: Well . . .

GUS: I believe you already said that.

(NELLIE BESS *laughs.*)

THURMOND: Aw hail, I'm just tryin' to say it's real good to have you home . . . Miss Sparkles.

(NELLIE BESS *claps her hands to her cheeks.*)

NELLIE BESS: Oh, my God! Nobody has called me that since I don't know *when.*

THURMOND: *I* know when!

NELLIE BESS (*flustered*): Ah, well, ah . . . what's the latest local gossip?

THURMOND (*teasing*): Ain't been a sprig of gossip since you left town!

NELLIE BESS: Oh, *you!* What are we gonna do with him, Gus?

GUS: If he'd break a leg we could shoot him.

> (NELLIE BESS *laughs, too loudly and too abruptly, and just as abruptly breaks it off. Another long, long beat.*)

NELLIE BESS: So! How did the mighty Stanley High Jackrabbits do last football season?

THURMOND: Just as sorry as *puke!*

GUS: The boy's a poet, ain't he?

THURMOND: No kiddin', Nellie Bess, I don't think the Jackrabbits has won a dozen games all-told since me and you was in school. Best they done last year was *tie* Grandfalls! Hailfar, when I was playin' we run through Grandfalls like a dose a salts.

NELLIE BESS: You still go to all the games?

THURMOND (*grinning*): Oh, yeah, I still got a lotta Jackrabbit in me. Me and Buel Rapp carries the first-down chain at the home games. That gits us in free.

NELLIE BESS: That's . . . good.

THURMOND (*hastily*): 'Course, that ain't why we *do* it. I mean, hail, we could pay like everybody else. We just . . . civic-minded is all.

NELLIE BESS: That's . . . nice.

(They drink beer. Another long beat.)

THURMOND: You recollect ol' Buel Rapp, don't you?

NELLIE BESS (*smiling*): Now how could I forget the dumbest boy in the history of Stanley High? I'm afraid we called the poor guy "Dumb-Dumb" right to his face!

THURMOND: Yeah, when he come out for football he put his helmet on *first* and then tried to jam his shoulder pads over it!

(They laugh.)

Ol' Buel always was about three bricks shy of a load.

NELLIE BESS: What in the world is old "Dumb-Dumb" doing these days to keep body and soul together?

THURMOND (*uncomfortable*): Well, uh, he . . . he works over at the service station. (*A beat.*) With me.

NELLIE BESS: Oh.

(They drink beer in a long, tense silence. NELLIE BESS suddenly consults her wristwatch.)

Oh, God, Mama's gonna skin me alive! I promised to take her out to the cemetery to visit Daddy's grave and she's probably standing on her head!

(*She jumps off the barstool.* THURMOND *stares straight ahead and suddenly guzzles his beer.*)

NELLIE BESS: Sure good to see you, Thurmond.

THURMOND (*brooding*): Yeah.

GUS: Now don't be a stranger to this place, Nellie Bess, ya hear?

NELLIE BESS: I promise! 'Bye now. And thanks for the beer, Thurmond.

THURMOND (*not looking at her*): Don't mention it.

(NELLIE BESS *hesitates for a beat, then rapidly exits.* THURMOND *turns up his beer and chug-a-lugs it dry, then slams the empty bottle on the bar.*)

THURMOND: I reckon you heard what that high-hat little bitch said to me!

GUS (*flaring*): Don't you cuss her! You ain't good enough for her to wipe her feet on.

THURMOND: Well for damn sure that's what *she* thinks!

GUS: Oh, balls! You go around wearin' a chip on your shoulder big enough to of been passed by a giant buffalo.

THURMOND: You didn't hear her trap me into admittin' I work alongside the dumbest sumbitch in Carlton County?

GUS: It wadn't deliberate! And if you do, whose fault *is* that? You ain't shackled to them damn gas pumps.

THURMOND: Just drop it, Gus!

(G U S *moves away and wipes at the bartop with a rag, grumbling.*)

G U S (*after a beat*): Before you seen Nellie Bess and come down with lockjaw, what was it you busted in here to tell me?

T H U R M O N D: Well shit, I couldn't hardly tell it in fronta her! Her and her old man has split up!

G U S: Know that for a fact, do you?

T H U R M O N D: Hail yes! Her own mama was talking about the disgrace of it this mornin' in the damn post office. That old woman don't hold with divorce.

G U S: Shit. Divorce is our most civilized custom! But how you know them kids ain't just tryin' one of them trial separations?

T H U R M O N D: The old lady never cottoned to that Cisco bone-twister. Miz Powers always hoped Nellie Bess would marry me.

(*He reaches over and claims the remainder of the beer* N E L L I E B E S S *had been drinking.*)

G U S: Well, if that's true—

T H U R M O N D: It is!

G U S: —a old woman that sees Jesus fartin' around this two-holer town half the time likely ain't accountable.

T H U R M O N D: Did Nellie Bess mention anythang about leavin' her old man?

G U S: Naw.

THURMOND (*suspicious*): Then what'd y'all talk about?

GUS: The International Monetary System.

THURMOND: Shit! (*A beat.*) She say anythang about me?

GUS: She more or less agreed you're likely to lay around this dump 'til you turn to a tub of clabber.

THURMOND: Oh she did, did she? Well I might just surprise you *and* Little Miss High Hat one of these days.

GUS: I've heard the wind blow before.

THURMOND: You think you can just look at somebody and see what's in their head, don't you? See right through their hair and their skull and their brain just like goddamn Superman! Well lemme tell ya: You don't know shit from shoe polish about me! I got some plans you couldn't guess if you was on a quiz show! Oh, maybe I ain't worked out all the little details yet. But I will, I will. You just hide and watch me.

(GUS *shakes his head;* THURMOND *stands, reaches in his pockets and produces several quarters.*)

Gimme some damn jukebox dimes.

GUS (*making change*): Whose piggy bank you rob?

THURMOND (*furious*): Don't be sayin' that about me! That ain't nothin' to joke about!

GUS (*taken aback*): Well . . . I . . . just couldn't help wonderin' how a feller that didn't have a copper cent yesterday all of a sudden sprouted two pocketfuls of quarters.

Playwright Larry L. King as saloon-keeper Gus Gilbert watches reunion of Nellie Bess Powers Clark (Elizabeth DuVall) and Thurmond Stottle (Mark W. Johnson) in the Washington production of Hank Williams *at New Playwrights' Theatre. (Photo by Dick Swanson)*

Moon Childers (Grady Smith) celebrates his domino superiority over a grim Gus Gilbert (Larry L. King) in the Washington New Playwrights' run. Smith appeared in the Washington, Texas, and Orpheum Theatre (New York) productions. (Photo by Dick Swanson)

Sheriff Royce Landon, Jr. (Greg Procaccino) gets on Thurmond's case (Mark W. Johnson) as Nellie Bess (Elizabeth DuVall) shows concern in the Washington production. (Photo by Dick Swanson)

Thurmond Stottle (Gabriel Folse) sings to an appreciative Nellie Bess Powers Clark (Christine Poole) in the Live Oak Theatre production in Austin. (Photo by Carol Felauer)

Gus Gilbert (Lou Perry) tries to strike sparks from the past with an unrelenting Vida Powers (Jill Parker-Jones) in the Austin production. (Photo by Carol Felauer)

In Austin, Nellie Bess (Christine Poole) says good-bye to Gus (Lou Perry) as Moon Childers (Grady Smith) attempts to comfort her. (Photo by Carol Felauer)

Thurmond Stottle (Matt Mulhern) and Gus Gilbert (Darren McGavin)
reminisce about Thurmond's glory days as a high school football star in
the Orpheum Theatre production in New York. (Photo by Martha Swope)

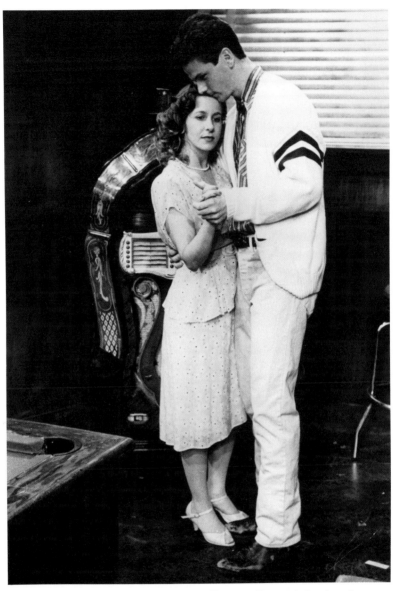

In the Orpheum Theatre production, Nellie Bess (Betsy Aidem) and Thurmond (Matt Mulhern) try to recapture the mood of their high school courting days, dancing to the jukebox in Gus Gilbert's bar. (Photo by Martha Swope)

THURMOND: Maybe I won it in a poker game.

GUS: Shit! I've seen you bet into a pair of Aces *showin'*.

THURMOND: Well maybe a rich uncle died and left me a whole shitpot fulla money! Whatta you care, you takin' the Census?

(He whirls and stalks to the jukebox.)

GUS *(looking after him)*: Son, I'd be real careful not to git on the bad side of Tood Brandon. That old cuss is mean to the bone, and he'd die for his money quicker'n he'd die for the flag.

(A beat; no response.)

If Tood Brandon ever suspicioned you was puttin' anything over on him, he'd turn on you like a mad dog.

THURMOND *(his back still to GUS)*: I don't recollect ever appointin' you my goddamn guardian.

GUS *(losing patience)*: Well you bein' so damned independent all of a sudden, and havin' more money than a truck load of Rockefellers, maybe you'd like to settle the tabs you owe me.

THURMOND *(punching his jukebox selection)*: Damn whistlin'!

(He whirls to face GUS.)

Just tell me how much, Old Man!

GUS: Two dollars and a damn dime!

(We hear, VO, a country-western song as THURMOND stalks to the bar and slaps down eight quarters and a dime: whap! whap! whap! whap! *through nine coins. GUS grabs each coin*

*as it hits and tosses it into his cash register. Then he takes
the signed tabs from his billfold and flings them on the bar.*
THURMOND *grabs the tabs, tears them into tiny pieces and
is ostentatiously scattering the resulting debris on the bartop
at . . .)*

BLACKOUT

Act I/Scene 3

Lights come up on the barroom. GUS *sits alone at the domino table, studying the dominoes in his hand as he takes a bite of chili from an open can. The chair across from* GUS *is empty, but three dominoes facing away from* GUS—*and a half-finished beer— make it apparent a game is in progress and the hand has been interrupted. A pattern of dominoes already played snakes across the table. A half-dozen others are face down in the "boneyard."*

GUS (*calling*): Moon, did you fall in?

MOON (*offstage*): Job like this can't be rushed!

GUS (*grumbling*): Looks like the son-of-a-buck could of helt his water 'til this hand was over.

(*After a beat,* MOON *enters from the men's room, buttoning up. He wears coveralls. The words "AUNT CLARA'S BAKERY" are stitched across the back.*)

MOON (*entering*): Man, I taken a pee that was better'n young love.

GUS: You been in there so long I thought maybe you'd fell in love with yourself.

MOON: It was just a mild flirtation. (*As he sits.*) I still say if you'd *give* your beer away and charge a dollar to piss, you'd make more money.

(MOON *takes a drink of beer as* GUS *spoons another mouthful of chili from the can.*)

43

GUS: You ever notice chili don't taste as good as it used to?

MOON: Don't nothin' taste as good as it used to.

GUS: A man gits old and his taste buds can't tell him the difference between flapjacks and cattle fodder.

MOON: If you didn't smoke like a damn barbecue pit, you could taste your food.

GUS (*giving him a look*): You a doctor now, as well as a economics expert?

MOON: Some folks thinks chili tastes better out of a bowl.

GUS: Cans heat better on my hotplate and I don't have to wash 'em. Moon, goddern it, play.

MOON: Your memory's gettin' as bad as your taste buds. It's your play.

GUS (*studying him*): You tryin' to trick me?

MOON: Naw. It ain't necessary.

(GUS *plays a domino and marks himself a fifteen count.*)

In a pig's ass, Gus! You can't do that!

GUS: What you whinin' about, Moon? Ten and five makes fifteen where I went to school.

MOON: I don't give a flip if you went to Harvard, that double-four you played on ain't the spinner! The double-blank is the spinner!

GUS: You sure?

MOON: Hail yes and you oughta be! You set it!

GUS (*reclaiming the misplayed domino*): Awright, if you're gonna be a damn crybaby.

MOON: And don't forget to erase that count you marked yourself.

GUS (*seemingly astonished*): I never marked myself a count.

MOON: The hail you never! You played on a spinner that *wadn't* a spinner and then marked yourself a fifteen count! Now erase it, Gus, this here's the rubber game!

(GUS, *grumbling, erases marks from the table top.*)

You likely to wind up eatin' that four-five, now that you went and exposed it tryin' to cheat.

GUS (*playing another domino*): Moon, if bullshit was money you'd be richer'n the Fort Worth stockyards. Now hush your monkey chatter and play.

MOON (*doing so immediately*): Awright, but it'll cost you a ten count.

(GUS *shakes his head in exasperation, marks the count, and himself plays another rock.* MOON *studies the board, hitting the table with one of his dominoes several times as he cogitates.*)

GUS (*after several beats*): Don't take all day, Moon! *I* can't deliver two dozen loaves of Aunt Clara's sourdough and call it a goddern work day.

MOON (*playing and grinning*): How you fixed for blanks?

G U S: I'll be dipped in shit!

(He draws four dominoes from the boneyard before getting one he can play.)

G U S *(as he draws)*: You the *luckiest* man since Lazarus.

(He plays a domino. M O O N *immediately plays his last rock, smacking it down forcefully on the table.)*

M O O N: Domino and out! That's another dollar you owe me!

(G U S *stares at the board in astonishment for a beat, rises, takes a dollar from his pocket and tosses it on the table.* M O O N *scoops up the dollar and quickly pockets it.)*

G U S: If you're gonna keep on robbin' me, Moon, it'd help my pride if you'd carry a gun.

M O O N: I teach a beginners' course Tuesday nights at the Odd Fellows Hall. Might help your game to enroll.

G U S: Well justice would be a heap better served if you'd beat Tood Brandon outta twenty bucks a week, instead of a poor bugger like me.

M O O N: Wouldn't be worth it. Tood's so stingy he won't play for no more'n a dime a game.

G U S: The old bastard owns everything in town but the water tower and he *still* ain't satisfied.

M O O N: And even if I win a dime from him, I hafta put up with about fifty dollars worth of his Republican crapola. *(Laughs.)* Tood's tellin' it that unless General Ike wins the election and saves them oil Tidelands for Texas, we're all goin' to hell in gunnysacks. He claims Adlai Stevenson's likely to give the Tidelands to the Communists and the New York Jews.

GUS: Don't make no difference to me who owns them damn Tidelands. All the oil *I* got's in my crankcase or on my hair.

MOON: Tood told me, "Moon, keepin' the Tidelands for Texas is *bound* to put money in your pocket one way or another."

GUS: That's a crock!

MOON: I said, "Tell you what, Tood: When they bring my first batch, I'll give my notice to Aunt Clara!"

(They laugh.)

GUS: Well they say everbody's got their good side. But I've walked plumb around Tood Brandon a thousand times and still ain't found his.

MOON: Hail, he don't even pay Thurmond Stottle enough that the boy can afford to file for bankruptcy!

(THURMOND, wearing his Gulf station uniform, rushes in; on seeing MOON, he stops dead in his tracks.)

MOON: Speak of the devil and he'll show up. *(To THURMOND.)* We was just talkin' about you.

THURMOND *(suspiciously)*: What about me?

MOON *(pretends to think; then, to GUS)*: You recollect?

GUS *(also pretending to think)*: Naw. Guess it wadn't important enough.

THURMOND (*sarcastically*): You two comedians oughta be on the radio.

MOON (*looking at his watch*): Why it ain't nowheres near your quittin' time, Thurmond. Who's mindin' the store?

THURMOND: If it's any of your bidness, I left Buel Rapp in charge for a minute.

MOON: Jesus Christ, couldn't you a-found a small blind child?

THURMOND: Well I *had* a private matter to talk over with you, Gus. But I guess it can wait.

MOON: Naw, go on ahead with it. I gotta finish my rounds for Aunt Clara. See you boys.

(MOON *exits*. THURMOND *waits until he's sure* MOON *is gone.*)

THURMOND: Gus . . . Nellie Bess come in for gas today. First time I'd seen her since in here a week ago. But she didn't really *need* gas, all I done was top her tank. And she was real friendly, so . . . well, I figgered she was wantin' to git together with me. Like old times.

GUS: That's how you figgered it, huh?

THURMOND: Well I musta been right! She's meetin' me over in Kermit tonight.

GUS: I could of gone the whole summer without needin' to know that.

THURMOND: What's wrong with two old friends goin' to a picture show and . . . maybe eatin' a steak?

G U S: If you're so damned innocent, why you sneakin' off to meet like you're plottin' to rob a bank?

T H U R M O N D: You want us to advertise on a billboard?

G U S: That girl's troubled right now, Thurmond. She ain't thinkin' clear. It don't become you to try to take advantage.

T H U R M O N D: Gus . . . behind all that sweet and purty, Nellie Bess is the toughest person I know. Anybody thinks they can take advantage of her's likely to draw back a nub.

G U S: Hope you're right. For a change.

T H U R M O N D (*impatient*): Anyhow, what'd I come by for—could you let me hold a few bucks 'til payday?

G U S (*suspiciously*): How few?

T H U R M O N D: Say . . . twenny-fie bucks?

G U S: Damn! You aim to fly her to Las Vegas?

T H U R M O N D: Hail, Gus, I just don't wanta run short in front of Nellie Bess! I'll bring back what I don't spend. This is damned important to me.

(G U S *studies him, undecided.*)

It's important to her too, Gus! Her mama's drivin' her flatdab crazy and she needs a break.

(G U S *sighs, produces his billfold and counts out money.*)

G U S: This is due me Friday without fail.

THURMOND: You won't be sorry, Gus.

GUS: I'll be *damned* sorry if that gal decides to hang around this hellhole on account of you.

THURMOND (*pocketing cash and grinning*): If you wanta preach, why don't you buy yourself a tent and some foldin' chairs?

GUS: Go on! Git your worthless bones outta here. And try to behave yourself tonight.

(THURMOND *grins, tosses him a salute, turns to exit, and almost collides with* SHERIFF ROYCE LANDON, JR., *who enters all cocky swagger on which is imposed a dead-eyed good-old-boy fake good humor.*)

SHERIFF LANDON: What's your hurry, Stottle? You just rob this place and tryin' to make your getaway?

THURMOND: Uh . . . naw.

SHERIFF LANDON: Seems like you're always rushin' from here to yonder in a big sweat. But all that motion don't seem to *git* you noplace. You ever stop to think about that?

THURMOND: Naw.

SHERIFF LANDON: Reminds me of some ol' chicken that's had its neck wrung. Floppin' around all over the place, jumpin' up in the air, doublin' back. And all for *nothin'*. 'Cause no matter how much it flops and jumps, that ol' chicken's gonna wind up down in the dirt. (*A beat.*) You know what that chicken needs, Stottle?

THURMOND: I . . . guess not.

SHERIFF LANDON: Why, what that chicken needs is a sense

of *di*-rection! So it won't just flop around to no good purpose. (*A beat.*) You reckon that's what *you* need, Stottle?

THURMOND (*after a long beat*): Can I go now?

SHERIFF LANDON (*seemingly surprised*): Why . . . *sure!* It's a free country, ain't it?

(THURMOND *edges by the* SHERIFF *and darts out the door.* SHERIFF LANDON *grins at his back before turning to* GUS.)

I'd sure hate to be in your bidness, Gus. (*A beat.*) Man runnin' a place like this, he's purty much got to put up with whatever . . . *trash* comes through his door.

GUS (*levelly*): I was thinkin' that very same thing.

SHERIFF LANDON (*shooting him a look*): Oh you was, was ya? (*A beat.*) Well, think about if you remember whether you've seen that Stottle boy flashin' money in here lately. (*A beat.*) Huh?

GUS (*after a beat*): Why you askin'?

SHERIFF LANDON (*with big humorless grin*): You know, Gus, I don't believe a real good upstandin' citizen would be askin' *me* why I'm askin' *him* questions in line with my official duties.

(*They engage in prolonged eye contact before the* SHERIFF *breaks it off, takes a cigar from his pocket and begins unwrapping it.*)

But, then, I don't suppose a real *good* citizen would of had his beer license suspended half-a-dozen times.

GUS (*quickly, angrily, in a rush*): Twice! Once a long time ago when your daddy squealed to the Liquor Control boys that I

was open ten minutes past legal hours . . . and a few months ago
you grabbed me for *givin'* a poor bugger a drink from my private
stock . . . after some drunk roughneck had put lumps on his head.

SHERIFF LANDON: Well now the *law* says that givin' away
hard liquor in a joint like this is just the same as sellin' it. (*A beat.*)
You askin' me to look past *the law?*

(GUS *turns away; the* SHERIFF, *lighting his cigar, eyes him.*)

You never have been friendly to me . . . or to my daddy durin' the
twenty-eight years he wore this same badge. Fact is, my daddy
says you always seemed to have your stinger out for *him* even way
back when y'all was schoolboys. And now you're treatin' *me* like a
stepchild. Now just why is that, Gus?

GUS (*giving him a look*): I never liked bullies, Junior, boy or man.

SHERIFF LANDON (*feigning surprise*): Oh is *that* what the
problem is? I just be damned! Just goes to show you how wrong a
man can be. I always thought—always *heard*—that maybe you
bowed your neck on account of my old daddy and you . . . well,
bein' sweet on the same girl way back yonder.

GUS: You wanta state your bidness?

SHERIFF LANDON (*grinning*): Why I thought I *had.* (*A beat.*)
'Course, now, the way that girl turned out . . . I reckon you and my
daddy both is lucky you didn't latch on to her permanent. All that
prayin' and Jesus-whoopin' she taken up later probably woulda got
on a man's nerves. From all I hear, the way she usta love snugglin'
up in the moonlight—

GUS (*quickly*): Thurmond ain't been flashin' no money. (*A beat.*)
He . . . borrowed a little dab from me just before you come in.

SHERIFF LANDON: You coulda saved us a lotta poker playin' if you'd told me that when I first asked.

GUS: Well now I've told you.

SHERIFF LANDON: But I wonder why you hesitated so long when I first asked? Just for a flicker there, I woulda swore I'd hit it smack on the nose.

(GUS *suddenly starts swabbing the bar with his cloth.*)

I thought I seen . . . a little somethin' stir in your eyes.

GUS: You flat wrong about that.

SHERIFF LANDON: Maybe. Maybe. *(A beat.)* I don't suppose you'd know if your friend Stottle has been makin' any moonlight runs? Late, unexplained meanderings?

GUS: Naw. And it ain't any of my bidness.

SHERIFF LANDON: Well now you *know* he got hisself mixed up in some kinda oil-field thievin' a couple years ago, right after I taken office.

GUS: I know you *accused* him of it. But the Grand Jury wouldn't indict him.

SHERIFF LANDON *(stung; nettled)*: Grand Juries can make mistakes like anybody else!

(A beat; he forces a grin.)

But, hell, that's spilt milk. No use to cry over it. Sooner or later, Thurmond's likely to step in deeper shit than he can walk in.

GUS: What's goin' on between you and him, anyway?

SHERIFF LANDON: Why . . . *(Laughs.)* . . . that's just what I was about to ask *you!* You know, Gus, it's always been a mystery to me how you seem to get so . . . well, so *close* to young people. Kinda . . . *cozy* with 'em. It don't seem—well, in a man your age, it just don't seem quite . . . natural. Not natural a-tall. *(A beat.)* Especially . . . when they're boys.

GUS *(giving him a long, hard look)*: Sheriff, if I didn't know that was just your chickenshit way of tryin' to git my goat . . . I might blow your ass away for that kinda slander.

SHERIFF LANDON: Ah . . . say again?

GUS: You heard me.

SHERIFF LANDON: Well I *thought* I just heard you *threaten* me!

GUS: I'd say it was more in the nature of damned strong advice.

SHERIFF LANDON: Well, I'll remember that. I *guarantee* you I'll remember it. Yessir.

(He puffs his cigar, takes it out of his mouth and slowly inspects it. Continues talking during cigar bit.)

This sure has been a disappointin' day. After you got suspended for fuckin' up that last time, and we come to a understandin' about me puttin' up a campaign poster in here, I kinda thought we had come to a understandin'. So I hadn't kept a particular hard eye on this shitty little joint. But now . . . well, now I just don't hardly know what to think.

GUS: Well while you're studyin' about it, why don't you take down your campaign poster? And take it with you.

NELLIE BESS: No reason it should.

THURMOND: I guess when a guy goes out with a Cisco girl he's supposed to figger she's seen the elephant and heard the owl.

NELLIE BESS: Thurmond! What's *that* supposed to mean?

(THURMOND *sullenly takes a hit of beer as the telephone rings.*)

GUS (*into telephone*): Sundowner. (*A beat.*) Naw, Sheriff, I hadn't seen him all night. (*A beat.*) Damn right I'm sure! You callin' me a liar? (*He listens for several beats.*) Well that's too bad. You know if he was hurt? (*A beat.*) 'Fraid I can't help you.

(*He hangs up the telephone and stares at* MOON.)

Just got tangled up in your own feet, did ya?

THURMOND: What's goin' on, Gus?

GUS: Seems like our friend Moon parked his car at a high rate of speed in the display window at Pioneer Furniture.

(THURMOND *laughs.*)

MOON: Hell I didn't have much choice after I bounced off that parkin' meter.

THURMOND (*laughing*): Hey, Moon, I thought you was tryin' to break yourself of trick drivin'!

(MOON *laughs and lifts his beer as if in a toast.*)

GUS: It ain't gonna be any laughin' matter if the Sheriff catches you drunk in here and me lyin' to protect you. Dammit, Moon, why'd you run off and leave your car parked in the wreckage?

MOON: One of my wheels got snared in a set of bedsprings.

(THURMOND *and* NELLIE BESS *laugh.*)

GUS (*taking off apron*): Come on, you old fool, I'll drive you out to the Highway Mo-Tel. The Sheriff's likely to stake out your house all night.

MOON: But that damn mo-tel's run by Baptists! They ain't even got a beer bar!

GUS: You think the county jail's got a beer bar?

(GUS *comes from behind the bar.*)

NELLIE BESS: Time out!

(*They all look at her.*)

Not meaning to butt in, but . . . well, wouldn't it make sense to go to the Sheriff's office and face the music sooner than later?

GUS: It *would* . . . if Moon wadn't silly drunk and the Sheriff wadn't serious crazy.

THURMOND: Yeah, Nellie Bess, and Moon cain't stand another drunk drivin' charge. One more and they've told him he cain't drive the bread truck no more.

MOON: By mornin' I'll be sober and can claim somebody *stole* my car tonight.

GUS (*taking* MOON *by the arm*): Let's make tracks, Party Boy.

MOON: Howza 'bout a fresh beer for the road?

GUS: Dammit, Moon, there ain't time!

(He tugs on MOON, *who lunges for the remainder of his beer and is dragged off carrying it.)*

GUS: I'd be obliged if you kids will hold down the fort 'til I git back.

*(*GUS *and* MOON *exit;* GUS *grumbling at him.)*

THURMOND: Wow! Looks like a hot time in the old town tonight.

NELLIE BESS: It's either Snoozeville or Dodge City around here. Never any in-between.

THURMOND *(smiling)*: Yeah, yeah. *(A beat.)* Uh, lissen, Nellie Bess . . . I'm sorry I give you a hard time about you already seein' that movie.

NELLIE BESS: I probably handled it wrong.

THURMOND: Naw, Nellie Bess, it seems like I'm always flyin' off the handle about the least little thang these days. I feel like I'm right on the edge of . . . fallin' offa somethin' high. *(A beat.)* And my music . . . I try real hard, Nellie Bess. Thump on that ol' guitar. Write songs and mail 'em to Nashville. But don't nothin' *happen!*

*(*NELLIE BESS *reaches over and touches his hand.)*

NELLIE BESS: Don't give up.

THURMOND: I even wrote ol' Hank Williams a personal letter a couple years ago. You know that?

NELLIE BESS: No!

THURMOND: Damn sure did! I asked him what to do to really git started in the music bidness and stuff. And you know what I got back?

NELLIE BESS: What?

THURMOND (*rising; agitated*): A autographed picture that'd been signed by a damn machine! I wet my finger and tested the ink and it never even smeared!

NELLIE BESS: Oh, that disappoints me in him!

THURMOND (*resigned*): Aw, it ain't Hank's fault. He's busy cuttin' records, makin' personal appearances with his band. I doubt Hank much more'n *seen* my letter. Probably he told some flunky to answer, and the flunky just sent that damn ol' picture.

 (*A beat; he sighs.*)

I dunno, just seems like I cain't git that first break . . .

NELLIE BESS: Breaks don't come hitchhiking down Highway 80 asking to be picked up, Thurmond. If you have a dream you've got to chase it.

THURMOND: Aw, I know. I wake up ever' mornin' knowin' I won't be no better off than when I went to bed. But, hailfar, seems like I cain't git far enough ahead to make it past the county line. Maybe if I could—

 (THURMOND *breaks off as* SHERIFF LANDON *enters.*)

SHERIFF LANDON (*after a hurried look around*): Where's Gus, Stottle?

THURMOND (*hesitating*): He . . . ain't here at the present.

SHERIFF LANDON: I can *see* that much! I asked you where he's *at*.

THURMOND: Uh . . . I dunno.

SHERIFF LANDON: Let's start from the beginning: Was he here when you come in?

NELLIE BESS (*quickly*): He said he had an errand to run, Sheriff. We didn't . . . pry.

SHERIFF LANDON (*feigning surprise*): Why hello there, Miz Clark! I didn't recognize you!

(*He takes off his hat in an exaggerated gesture of courtliness and grins widely.*)

Most likely that's because . . . well, I guess I more or less would of expected you to be with your husband. (*A beat.*) How is he, by the way?

NELLIE BESS: He's fine.

SHERIFF LANDON: Well that's real good to hear! Yessir, sure is. Ain't anything like a happy young couple in love. I can spot 'em at a thousand paces. Sure can. (*A beat.*) I guess you and Stottle just sorta happened to . . . bump into each other in here. That right?

THURMOND: Yeah. That's right.

SHERIFF LANDON: Well I guess you two old friends was just *destined* to bump into one another tonight. See, a little bit ago I was out yonder by the "Y"—where the Kermit and Monahans roads fork?—and I woulda nearly swore I seen Miz Clark's car pass and then not more'n a minute later I seen your old green wreck pass. Kind of a coincidence, ain't it?

THURMOND: I . . . reckon you could say that.

SHERIFF LANDON: Yeah, I reckon you could *say* that. *(A beat.)* Anything goin' on over in Monahans tonight?

THURMOND: I . . . I was in Kermit.

SHERIFF LANDON: Oh, *Kermit!* Well, shoot, that kinda disappoints me. Sheriff McNerlin over there in Monahans, he tells me he's losin' some tool cable to oil-field thieves. And I was gonna ask if you seen anything suspicious between here and there. You know—strange trucks, rough-lookin' strangers that mighta been makin' midnight requisitions.

THURMOND: Naw.

SHERIFF LANDON: Well, didn't hurt to ask. You might remember we had a run of oil-field thievin' in this country two, three years ago. You recollect that, Stottle?

THURMOND: Yeah.

SHERIFF LANDON: I kinda thought you might.

  (THURMOND *hides in his beer.*)

Miz Clark, I don't suppose *you* seen anything suspicious on the Monahans Road? Or was you in Kermit too?

NELLIE BESS *(giving him a look)*: Sheriff, I don't believe that's any of your concern.

SHERIFF LANDON *(exaggeratedly contrite)*: Oh, I'm sorry! I didn't mean to . . . *pry.* Any more than you pried into Gus's mysterious errand. *(A beat.)* And, again, I don't *pry* . . . but I wondered if maybe you'd seen Moon Childers tonight?

THURMOND (*too quickly*): Naw. Naw I ain't. Really ain't.

SHERIFF LANDON (*to* NELLIE BESS): I don't suppose you . . .?

(She shakes her head.)

So then you wouldn't know what *happened* to him tonight?

THURMOND: Naw.

SHERIFF LANDON (*to* NELLIE BESS): You?

NELLIE BESS: No.

SHERIFF LANDON (*after a long beat*): Well, ain't you even *curious* what mighta happened to him?

THURMOND: Uh, oh sure. Yeah. Uh, what mighta happened to him?

(SHERIFF LANDON *studies them for a moment, then grins.*)

SHERIFF LANDON: Naw. Naw, I won't burden you with it. Enjoy yourselves. (*A beat.*) And each other.

(He touches the brim of his hat in an exaggerated salute and exits.)

THURMOND (*rising*): That sorry sumbitch! Same as accusin' us of—

NELLIE BESS: Simmer down, Thurmond. He's just playing mean little games, hoping to get us all worked up.

THURMOND: Cain't nothin' go wrong within a hunnert miles of

here that he don't try to load on *my* back! And he sure ain't got any call to go insultin' *you* like that! It's a damn good thing he left when he did! I was right up against tellin' that sumbitch how the cow ate the cabbage!

NELLIE BESS: It would only have made trouble for you.

THURMOND: I still got it in my craw how he usta sniff around after you when me and you was goin' steady! If he didn't wear that badge and gun—

NELLIE BESS: He never got to first base with me, Thurmond. Which is probably one of the reasons he comes down on you so hard.

THURMOND (*sitting*): I used to love this little ol' town. There was a time when I couldn't hardly walk a block without people comin' up to slap me on the back and brag about how I'd done in our last football game. But people, dammit, they seem to of *changed!* Them same people that slapped me on the back, now they drive up for gas and look right through me. Like I ain't even there. (*A sigh.*)

NELLIE BESS: One thing for sure: We didn't know how easy we had it back in Dear Old Stanley High.

THURMOND (*brightening*): That's for damn sure! Why, back then, if I wadn't carryin' a football or hot-roddin' some old car, I thought my life was pure misery.

NELLIE BESS (*smiling*): Remember how upset you'd get when Coach Nooncaster kept us after school? For passing notes in study hall?

THURMOND: And made us memorize goddamn poetry!

NELLIE BESS: Oh, you hated that! (*Laughs.*) Want to see if you can still rip off a few choice lines of Kipling?

THURMOND (*grinning*): No, thanks, I'd druther set on a hot stove! (*Shakes his head.*) Coach Noon was a mighty good football man, but when it come to goddamn poetry you just couldn't *reason* with him. One time I said, "Coach, poetry ain't a thing in the world but songs without music and what good is *that?*"

NELLIE BESS (*smiling*): What did he say?

THURMOND (*frowning*): Well, I couldn't figger out why—but he called me a Philippine.

NELLIE BESS (*laughing*): Oh, Thurmond, I'll bet he called you a "Philistine"!

THURMOND (*suspiciously*): What's that mean?

NELLIE BESS: Somebody . . . well, somebody not real interested in cultural matters.

THURMOND (*relieved*): I'll be damned! And all this time I thought he'd insulted me.

(NELLIE BESS *laughs.*)

You know, Miss Sparkles . . . nothin' much has went right since you left town.

NELLIE BESS (*airily*): Oh, I don't think my leaving town meant much in the grand scheme.

THURMOND: It did to me.

(NELLIE BESS *maintains brief eye contact, then looks away.*)

Turned my whole life upside down.

NELLIE BESS (*to lighten mood*): My goodness, the way we're sitting around . . . philosophizing . . . you'd think we were a couple of deep-thinkers from Texas Tech!

THURMOND (*laughs*): Well, hail, let's quit the brainy stuff and dance one!

NELLIE BESS(*smiling*): Best offer I've had tonight.

THURMOND (*rising*): There you go!

(*He crosses to the jukebox, drops in a dime and punches a selection.* NELLIE BESS *rises and crosses to within a few feet of him. We hear,* VO, *a mournful country song.* THURMOND *turns to* NELLIE BESS *and she makes a mock curtsy; he responds with a brief, bobbing bow. They move together, dancing a bit apart, looking into each other's eyes as they do a slow, shuffling cowboy two-step.*)

[Here the first verse of a mournful country classic,
about ten lines long.]

(NELLIE BESS *nestles a bit closer; she places a hand, lightly, behind* THURMOND's *neck.*)

[Here about the next half dozen lines of the song.]

(THURMOND *pulls* NELLIE BESS *closer still; she smiles, closing her eyes, and places her head on his shoulder. They dance on, lost in some old dreamy remembrance.*)

[Here the next three lines of the song.]

(*They mutually pull back, looking deeply into each other's eyes.*)

[Here the final two lines of the song.]

(THURMOND *and* NELLIE BESS *engage in a fierce kiss at . . .*)

BLACKOUT
and
End of Act One

Act II/Scene 1

Ten days later. We hear from the dark a happy, bright, upbeat number. As lights come up on the main barroom, we see GUS *dusting off the blackboard surface of the domino table; a few empty or near-empty beer bottles on the bar make it clear he's still in his clean-up process. As song fades, there is a rough banging on the door.*

GUS: We ain't open yet! Come back in a hour!

THURMOND *(offstage)*: Gus, open up! It's me!

GUS: I don't care if it's Harry Truman! I ain't sellin' beer for a good hour and I ain't sellin' it on credit even then!

THURMOND *(offstage)*: Dang it, Gus, *Nellie Bess* is with me!

(GUS, *grumbling, crosses to open the door.* THURMOND, *in his off-duty cowboy clothes and carrying his guitar, enters; he is trailed by* NELLIE BESS, *dressed in tight white shorts, a bare-midriff halter top and sandals; she appears to be hanging back, as if reluctant to face* GUS.)

GUS: Well if it ain't the new Bonnie and Clyde!

THURMOND: Come on, Gus!

NELLIE BESS: I hope we're . . . not intruding.

GUS *(pretending to peer out the door)*: FBI followin' you?

THURMOND: Quit foolin' around, Gus!

GUS (*closing door*): Well, from everything I've been hearin', y'all becomin' nearly as no-torious as Bonnie and Clyde.

NELLIE BESS (*uncomfortable*): Well . . . you know . . . how small-town gossips carry on.

GUS: Yeah. And until lately I figured you did.

(*She looks away.*)

THURMOND: Uh, Gus, wonder if you'd mind if we borrowed your upstairs room for a few minutes?

(GUS *stares at* THURMOND *as if he has suddenly gone crazy.*)

GUS (*a spluttering outburst*): Well, goddog . . . if *that* don't take the goddern cake! Whatta ya think I'm runnin' here, Thurmond, a goddog hot-pillow mo-tel?

NELLIE BESS: It's not like you're making it *sound*, Gus! My God, have the gossips poisoned you too?

(*Now* GUS *looks away from her.*)

THURMOND: See, me and her's got a private matter to settle.

GUS: I guess I could pick up a few cans of chili and stop by the Post Office to pick up my bills. Fifteen, twenny minutes do it?

THURMOND: That'd be good.

NELLIE BESS: We appreciate it, Gus.

GUS (*not looking at her*): And I'd appreciate y'all confinin' your bidness to my downstairs here.

NELLIE BESS (*indignant*): Well *of course!*

GUS: And Thurmond . . . the beer box is *already* locked.

(*He exits.*)

NELLIE BESS (*staring after* GUS): I never thought I'd see the day Gus Gilbert would treat me like . . . yard goods.

THURMOND: Aw hail, Hon, don't worry about it. I think that ol' man's goin' through the change-of-life.

(*But* NELLIE BESS, *obviously hurt and puzzled, continues to stare at the door.* THURMOND *looks about, grabs a beer bottle from atop the bar and hurries back to replace it on the domino table. He begins unbuttoning his shirt as* NELLIE BESS *looks at him in wonder.* THURMOND *produces from inside his shirt a single red rose, by now a bit crumpled, straightens the stem and inserts the rose in the empty beer bottle. He becomes aware of* NELLIE BESS *staring at him.*)

THURMOND: I thought this bein' kind of a special occasion . . .

NELLIE BESS (*touched*): Why Thurmond Stottle! What a nice gesture!

THURMOND (*embarrassed*): Thank ye. (*A beat.*) I stole it outta Old Lady Livingston's flower bed.

NELLIE BESS: You . . . ? (*A hopeless little laugh.*) Did you have to tell me *that* part?

THURMOND: Well, I just . . . sorta done it on impulse. But now don't you worry, when my ship comes in I'm gonna buy you a whole truck loada roses. Ever' day!

(NELLIE BESS, *shaking her head, pulls a chair out from the table and sits; she fingers the rose as* THURMOND *props one foot on a chair and positions his guitar for playing.*)

THURMOND: Now the big moment's here, I'm nervous as a whore in church.

NELLIE BESS: Don't be silly! I'm on your side.

THURMOND: Now I don't want you sayin' you like it if you don't. That wouldn't gimme a fair test.

NELLIE BESS: I promise total honesty.

THURMOND: Well . . . hail . . . you don't have to go to no *extreme*. (*A beat.*) I mean, you don't hafta love it or hate it. You can, you know, just kinda like it fair to middlin'.

NELLIE BESS (*amused*): Sing, Thurmond.

(THURMOND *strums for a moment, then breaks off.*)

THURMOND: Goddamn, I'd give five dollars for a good cold beer!

NELLIE BESS: Sorry, Babe. Gus locked the beer box. Now sing!

THURMOND (*strumming, then again stopping*): How come your mama won't even keep a little wine around the house for Jesus? Bible says he drunk wine.

NELLIE BESS: Mama says the translation got it wrong, that it was just grape juice. Now sing your song.

(T H U R M O N D *again strums for a moment, and once more quits.*)

T H U R M O N D : What if you really like it, and we get all excited . . . and then it turns out it ain't worth a damn anyway?

N E L L I E B E S S : Will you please sing the damn song before I get too old and deaf to *hear* it?

T H U R M O N D : Okay, okay.

(He clears his throat, takes a deep breath, strums and begins to sing "I Keep Waking Up with Strangers." He is at first a bit uncertain, but better than we might have expected.)

T H U R M O N D (*singing*):

> I keep wakin' up with strangers
> With an oooold friend on my mind
> I keep courtin' mid-night dangers
> Not really carin' what I'll find.
> Then I quit each love-less lonely room
> When mornin' shows its pale, cold face
> But I keep wakin' up with strangers
> Who'll never take my old love's place.

N E L L I E B E S S : Thurmond! That's pretty!

(T H U R M O N D *grins, winks, and continues singing and strumming—but now with renewed confidence.*)

T H U R M O N D :

> Sometimes I close my eyes and whis-per
> A name that echoes from my past
> But I'm here to tell you mis-ter
> Old fadin' echoes never last.

I used to think that love was simple
But the simple fool was me
Now I keep wakin' up with strangers
In places I don't want to be.

Yeah I keep wakin' up with strangers
With an ooold friend on my mind
Learnin' love is less than useless
Unless that love's returned in kind.
And when the sun comes up tomorrow
I'll miss her feel of silk and lace
'Cause I keep wakin' up with strangers
Who'll always wear a stranger's face . . .

(*He runs his fanciest, lick-concluding guitar riff and looks at* NELLIE BESS *expectantly.*)

NELLIE BESS (*clapping her hands*): Bravo, Thurmond! That's really fine! I'm so proud of you!

THURMOND (*grinning widely*): It could stand a little tinkerin', but I guess I'm gettin' there. It ain't *quite* like I want it yet.

NELLIE BESS: "It isn't."

THURMOND (*alarmed*): It ain't what?

NELLIE BESS (*smiling*): "Isn't" quite like you want it. Not "ain't" quite like you want it.

THURMOND: Oh. Anyhow, I've thought up some damn good lines for another verse.

NELLIE BESS: Nice. Keep working on it.

(*She fingers the rose in the beer bottle, going away to some private place.*)

THURMOND (*enthused*): You know what my new song says to me?

NELLIE BESS (*idly*): What?

THURMOND: It says, "Thurmond Stottle, I'm a song needs to be sung by Eddie Arnold." (*A beat.*) Don't it sound like a Eddie Arnold song to you, Nellie Bess?

NELLIE BESS (*distracted*): I guess it could be . . .

THURMOND: Hail, I can close my eyes and just *hear* ol' Eddie Arnold singin' my song! Like we was in the same room! Singin' it . . . mellow and from the heart.

(*A beat; he dreams for a moment.*)

By God, soon as I git it all wrote I'm gonna mail the sumbitch to Eddie Arnold special delivery!

NELLIE BESS: "Written." Not "wrote."

THURMOND (*impatient*): Awright! (*A beat.*) You know, just one hit song sung by Eddie Arnold would open up near-about ever' door in Nashville to me, I bet. That's all it takes. Just one big hit and before he knows it a man can wind up lazy rich!

(*He wanders around a moment, still excited about his song, singing little snatches of it, snapping his fingers, then produc-ing a hollow sound by smacking alternate fists into alternate palms. Then he notices that* NELLIE BESS, *still fingering the rose, is distracted and staring into space. He starts creeping slowly and stealthily toward her. Then he suddenly leaps, grab-bing at her crotch and issuing a mighty shout.*)

THURMOND: *Woolly Buggar!*

NELLIE BESS: *Jesus Christ!*

(*As she leaps to her feet, her chair turns over;* THURMOND *breaks up, laughing and slapping his leg.*)

NELLIE BESS: My God, you scared me half out of my pants!

THURMOND: Just *half*? Then I better try again!

NELLIE BESS: Why don't you grow up?

(*But she issues a little half-smile as she rights the overturned chair.*)

THURMOND (*teasing*): I never heard no complaints about me not being growed up when we was parked out at the Sandhills. Or over in Odessa at that fancy eight-dollar mo-tel!

NELLIE BESS: *Thurmond!* If you're tryin' to get me run out of town, just take an ad in the *Carlton County Echo*.

(*He chuckles.*)

And it's "grown up," not "*growed* up."

THURMOND: Now dammit, Nellie Bess, you might be able to turn me into a rodeo clown or even into a tent preacher. But you'd just as well give up tryin' to make me a goddern English teacher!

NELLIE BESS (*sighing*): I must be crazy, getting mixed up with you again. You'll be murdering the English language and . . . pumping gas in this old town until Jesus comes back for real.

THURMOND (*hurt*): Nellie Bess, I sure do hope you're jokin'.

NELLIE BESS: I really don't know, Thurmond.

(She walks to the domino table and again fingers the bottled rose.)

Oh, I have a good time when I'm with you. I admit that. Time seems to turn back to when school dances and flirting in study hall were all that mattered, and tomorrow—well, if I even *thought* about tomorrow it was just a brain movie starring me and some handsome man who'd live happily ever after, like in a fairy tale. *(A beat.)* I'm a big girl now, Thurmond. I can't go on believing in fairy tales. *(A beat.)* Afterwards—after I leave you—I feel guilty . . . and rotten . . . and too sad to cry.

THURMOND: Well thank you a whole damn bunch!

(He turns his back and stalks to the jukebox, where he pretends to study the selections.)

NELLIE BESS *(turning to look at him)*: Thurmond, I *am* a married woman. *(A beat.)* Sort of. *(A beat.)* I didn't really intend . . . I suppose one night I had too many old memories, and more than I could handle of lonely and scared. I'm sorry, but when I stop to think things through, I just can't feel good about . . . what's happened. Anything we do today, Thurmond, walks with us into tomorrow.

(THURMOND whirls from the jukebox to face her; he is obviously nettled.)

THURMOND: You know what you remind me of?

NELLIE BESS: I'm afraid to risk a guess.

THURMOND: Some damned old fat person that eats like a *hog* and then whines about gainin' weight.

NELLIE BESS: Well now thank *you* a whole damn bunch!

(She now turns her back on him; THURMOND *walks from the jukebox toward her.)*

THURMOND: Naw, now, you just git down off of your high horse and think about it straight. When we're together you kick up your heels just as high as I do! You sing soprano just as loud as I sing bass! Dammit, woman, I ain't grabbed you by the hair of the head and *drug* you into no damn mc-tels!

NELLIE BESS: "Dragged" into "any."

THURMOND: Will you stop that schoolteacher crap and face the music? You wanta *dance,* Nellie Bess, you just don't wanta pay the fiddler!

(After a long beat, she turns to face him.)

NELLIE BESS: Thurmond, we have to think about conse-quences! *(A beat.)* I don't want to hurt anybody. *(A beat.)* And I don't think *you* do. *(A beat.)* Howard has faults, but I'm not out to hurt him. He's my husband and he's . . . a proud man.

THURMOND *(turning)*: Yeah? What's that bone-twistin' sum-bitch got to be so proud of?

*(*NELLIE BESS *gives him a long look.)*

NELLIE BESS *(softly)*: Well, now, it surely couldn't be *me* . . . could it?

THURMOND: Aw, now, that wadn't what I meant, Hon! *(A beat.)* I know all this ain't easy on you. Or for me, neither. *(A beat.)* When I was a little kid . . . and Christmas come . . . I knew that after the tree was took down . . . and the turkey and dressin' was all gone . . . that thangs would go back to bein' the same old hard-scrabble. Hard work and baloney sandwiches and broke toys. *(A beat.)* Christmas always seemed like a goddern *fake* to me, like the one day a year they give you to try and fool you outta your misery. *(A beat.)* But you knew all the time they was gonna snatch it back. *(A beat.)* Mama used to say, "Life don't give no double-your-money-back guarantees, Son! You gotta enjoy what you got *right now!" (A beat; shaking his head.)* Boy, it took me a long time . . . but I learnt to do that. To take "right now" and just *wallow* in it, 'cause even if they could mess you up tomorrow there wadn't no way they could rob you of "right now." Not unless you let 'em. *(A beat.)* Let's just enjoy what we got right now, Nellie Bess. While we *got* it.

(*She turns to him and touches his arm.*)

NELLIE BESS: I don't mean to take things out on you, Thurmond. I just feel under . . . such a strain. It's no fun being the town outcast . . .

THURMOND: No matter what your mama says . . . and no matter what anybody else says . . . you know I love you, Miss Sparkles.

(*He moves forward, takes her by the arms as if to kiss her, but she moves quickly away.*)

NELLIE BESS: Please don't say that! I can't afford to say it back.

THURMOND: Dammit, Nellie Bess, it just seems *right!* I can't help but say it.

NELLIE BESS: Be real sure what your heart feels, Thurmond—*real* sure—before you say that to me again.

THURMOND: Hell, Nellie Bess, I ain't playin' games. *(A beat.)* I went to the trouble to steal you that rose, didn't I?

(NELLIE BESS *chuckles and they briefly embrace; they spring apart just as* VIDA POWERS *enters at a brisk walk; she stops dead on seeing the couple.* NELLIE BESS *is obviously flustered.*)

NELLIE BESS: *Mama!* What are you doing *here?*

MRS. POWERS: I might ask you the same question. And with more justification.

NELLIE BESS: Oh . . . well . . . Thurmond was just playing his new song for me. It's real pretty.

THURMOND: Uh . . . hidy . . . Miz Powers . . .

MRS. POWERS: I've always heard an idle mind is the devil's workshop. Do you have a *job?*

THURMOND: Uh, yessum. But I get off Tuesday mornin' and all day Sunday. (*A beat.*) Today's, uh . . . Tuesday.

NELLIE BESS: She knows what day it is, silly.

MRS. POWERS: I don't think I like what I'm seeing here.

NELLIE BESS: Mama! What in the world are you talking about?

MRS. POWERS: It's not *me* doing the talking in this town! I hear reports that a certain couple has been seen parking at night out by the Sandhills State Park—

THURMOND (*abruptly*): Nellie Bess, I got to go!

MRS. POWERS: —in a old green 1941 Hudson Terrapin—

THURMOND (*grabbing guitar; leaving; calling back*): I promised my mom on a stacka Bibles to run some errands!

MRS. POWERS (*calling after him*): —with Stanley High Jackrabbit bumper stickers plastered all over it!

NELLIE BESS: Mama!

MRS. POWERS (*rushing to door; calling down the street*): And the only Bible *you* ever seen, Thurmond Stottle, was probably in some cheap sinner's motel!

NELLIE BESS: Mama, I hate it when you do that.

MRS. POWERS (*whirling to her*): And what do you think *I* hate, Miss Priss? Oh, I'm a Christian woman and I try *not* to hate, but maybe some awful things a Christian has a *duty* to hate. I hate seein' my only child shame her Dear Dead Daddy's name and rub her mama's nose in it.

NELLIE BESS (*hands over her ears*): Mama, don't start!

MRS. POWERS: I raised you in the Kingdom, child! I taught you to say "Je-Zus" before you could walk or wave bye-bye! I had you in the Sunbeams recitin' scriptures before you could read and led you to accept Jesus Christ when you was five years old! And to rededicate your life to the Lord twenty-two times before you even needed a brassiere!

NELLIE BESS: *And I hated it!*

MRS. POWERS (*aghast*): Don't . . . you . . . dare!

NELLIE BESS (*losing control*): Yes, Mama, I hated everything about it! The way you dragged me from house-to-house, witnessing for Jesus, getting a foot in the door pretending to sell your damned Avon products! You weren't selling polishes and lotions and soaps! You were selling circus tickets to a . . . a Holy Ghost freak show!

MRS. POWERS: The Lord will strike you down!

NELLIE BESS: *And you would love it, wouldn't you?*

(MRS. POWERS *rushes* NELLIE BESS *and grabs her by one arm.*)

MRS. POWERS: On your knees, girl!

NELLIE BESS (*resisting*): *No!*

MRS. POWERS: Get on your knees! Ask the Lord to forgive your blasphemous tongue!

(NELLIE BESS *attempts to loosen her mother's grip, but* MRS. POWERS *twists one of her arms so that* NELLIE BESS *does, indeed, fall to her knees.*)

MRS. POWERS: Pray, child! Pray for forgiveness and your holy redemption!

(NELLIE BESS *in one desperate lunge breaks her mother's grip, scrambles to her feet and faces her.*)

NELLIE BESS: You're sick, Mama! You're a crazed old woman who's done meaner things in the name of love than I'll *ever* do!

MRS. POWERS (*reaching out*): Nellie Bess—

NELLIE BESS: You've seen the last of me!

(NELLIE BESS *turns and exits at a run;* MRS. POWERS *swiftly moves toward the door.*)

MRS. POWERS (*calling*): Come back, Nellie Bess! You're jumping into Hellfire eternal! Come back!

(She abruptly stops screeching, but is obviously agitated. She takes a white handkerchief from her purse and, as if scrubbing away sins, begins to scour everything she walks by: a table, the bar, whatever. We hear her emitting deep, shaky breaths, and little moans; her lips move as if in prayer. She begins singing, at first labored, then gaining in strength as the words comfort her and she begins to settle down.)

MRS. POWERS *(singing)*:

> O my swee-eet precious Jesus
> My reason to live . . .
> My Mas-ter
> My Sav-iour
> My life I will give . . .

(She stops, struggling, then resumes in a fuller voice.)

> To work for Your glory
> Tell the wonderful story
> To sinners adrift
> On far shouls . . .
> Unknowing,
> Not caring,
> That my Je-Zus
> Can uplift their souls.

(She collects herself, puts away the handkerchief, checks her appearance and seems to regain a peaceful repose. GUS *enters; on seeing* MRS. POWERS *he is so startled that he drops a small bag containing cans of chili.)*

GUS: *Jesus Christ!*

MRS. POWERS: I see you haven't changed your blasphemous ways.

GUS: Well you'll have to excuse me, Vida. I wasn't exactly expectin' you as the day's first customer.

(He scrambles to pick up the chili.)

Well . . . have a seat, Vida.

MRS. POWERS: This will be fine.

GUS: Suit yourself.

MRS. POWERS: It wasn't easy for me . . . coming into this . . .

GUS: "Den of iniquity?"

MRS. POWERS: Your words, Mister Gilbert.

GUS: Oh, cut the crap, Vida. I've danced the cowboy stomp with you more'n once.

MRS. POWERS: I didn't come here to talk ancient history.

GUS *(with a small smile)*: I guess it qualifies as that, alright. *(A beat.)* What *did* you come in for, to take a hatchet to my bar stock?

MRS. POWERS *(after a beat)*: It's about Nellie Bess. I wouldn't trouble you . . . but she's hurt me bad. Her own mother.

GUS: Before you squat on your pity pot, Vida, maybe you oughta reflect on the Christian charity you've laid on her.

MRS. POWERS *(sharply)*: Hear me out, Gus! *(Quieter.)* I'd hoped I could talk to you . . . as an old friend.

GUS: Awright, Vida. But do me the favor of takin' a seat. I ain't comfortable standin' around like we're gettin' ready to fight a duel.

(She nods and crosses to the nearest chair, though she perches on its edge as if poised for flight.)

MRS. POWERS: I'm afraid Nellie Bess has some fool notion of going off with Thurmond Stottle. To my mind that's a terrible sin, a mortal—

GUS *(holding up a restraining hand)*: No profit in gettin' into all that stuff, Vida!

MRS. POWERS: Well, sin or not, it won't work! For all her faults, Nellie Bess is a cut above that . . . in-fidel roughneck. I've prayed and prayed over it, but the Lord must be usin' my daughter to test my faith. The Bible says He moves in mysterious ways—

GUS: Vida! This ain't a cathedral! And I ain't settin' in no pew waitin' for deliverance!

MRS. POWERS: Well maybe—

GUS *(cutting her off)*: And don't tell me I oughta be! *(Grumbling.)* Be *dogged* if I can figger how a girl that was the best saddle-horse barrel rider and square dancer in the county could of turned into a . . . Polly Parrot for Jesus. *(A beat.)* You used to *laugh*, Vida!

MRS. POWERS: Conditions change. People change. Their . . . hearts change.

GUS: Well "amen" to *that*, Sister! *(Sighs.)* Oh, hell, go ahead with what you got to say. Don't mind me.

MRS. POWERS: I'm asking you to persuade Nellie Bess against going off with him. She seems to listen to you more than most. Not that I've ever understood why . . .

GUS: Maybe it's because I talk to her instead of preachin' to her.

Listenin' is a big part of talkin', Vida, and I never met a preacher yet that could hear it thunder—unless he was makin' the rumble.

MRS. POWERS: If I preach it's because of my duty to my daughter. To see that she don't make the early mistakes I made.

GUS: Vida, we could argue all day if your biggest mistake was made sooner or later. But I reckon that'd require you to gimme some answers you wouldn't gimme more'n twenty-five years ago.

MRS. POWERS (*rising, after a long beat*): I know you think I'm just . . . a crazy old woman. But if you can see your way clear to help, I'll be much obliged.

GUS: Well, but . . . unnerstand I can't give you no guarantees.

MRS. POWERS (*nodding*): I thank you. (*A beat.*) I'm asking for Nellie Bess more than for me. You always seemed to have a special feeling for her. Sending birthday gifts and all . . . from when she was just a little toddler.

GUS: Well . . . I always thought that maybe I had good grounds for doing that.

(*They make eye contact for a long beat.*)

MRS. POWERS: God bless you . . . Gus.

(*She turns and rapidly exits.* GUS *stares after her as lights dim to . . .*)

BLACKOUT

Act II/Scene 2

From the dark we hear the sound track of a war movie: big guns, small arms fire, shouts, aircraft. A spotlight comes up on a cut-away front view of the interior of a car at a drive-in movie theater; a car speaker hangs from the window to THURMOND*'s immediate left.* THURMOND *and* NELLIE BESS *look out over the audience as if watching a drive-in movie screen. She wears shorts, a blouse, sandals, and her hair is tied up in a kerchief.* THURMOND *wears his usual scruffy off-duty cowboy outfit.* THURMOND *is behind the steering wheel, gobbling popcorn and very much lost in the action on the screen. Beside him* NELLIE BESS *is glum and restless. She shifts in the seat as* THURMOND *becomes more involved in the picture.*

THURMOND *(to movie screen)*: Watch that sumbitch behind you! *(A beat.)* To ya left, ya left!

> *(*NELLIE BESS *leans across him and cuts off the speaker; the sound track is no longer heard.)*

THURMOND *(startled)*: What the hail you doin', Hon? This is just gettin' good!

(He turns the speaker up and we again briefly hear the sounds of battle. NELLIE BESS *again leans across him to turn the speaker off.)*

NELLIE BESS: Thurmond! I want to talk!

THURMOND: Well go ahead and talk. I can listen to you and watch the show too.

NELLIE BESS: No! This is important enough for your undivided attention.

THURMOND (*irritated*): Why ain't women satisfied unless they can *talk* everthang to death? Men just go ahead and *do* thangs, but a damn woman's gotta poke at everthang and torment it.

NELLIE BESS (*sighing*): You sound more like a husband every day.

THURMOND: Well I ain't anybody's husband and maybe you oughta quit talkin' to me like I am!

NELLIE BESS: If that's an invitation to go my own way, I just might take you up on it.

THURMOND: Aw . . . you know better'n that.

NELLIE BESS: No, I don't. One minute you're ready to leave with me and try Nashville, and the next minute it's more important to you to see if John Wayne can win World War Two again. We'll never settle our problems if we don't talk them out.

THURMOND: Nellie Bess, you've talked 'til my ears has turned blue but it don't seem to git us anywheres.

NELLIE BESS: It might if you'd really listen and participate! But no! When we have a so-called "talk" you just grunt and look off in the distance with your eyes glazed over. And things rock along in the same old way.

THURMOND: Now that ain't true, Nellie Bess! Lately I've wrote two songs that you admit to bein' purty damn good.

NELLIE BESS: But what *good* are they kicking around in an old cigar box in Stanley, Texas? For Christ sake, Thurmond, do you think Eddie Arnold's likely to come down here and wrestle you for them?

(She moves across the seat, away from him, folds her arms and stares straight ahead.)

THURMOND *(after a long beat)*: I can turn the sound up if you're watchin' the movie.

NELLIE BESS: I am *not* watching the goddamn movie!

THURMOND: Nellie Bess, you know I cain't abide hearin' a woman cuss.

NELLIE BESS: Oh just go to hell!

(She turns her head away, bites the back of her hand and softly cries.)

THURMOND *(shifting uncomfortably)*: Now, Nellie Bess, that ain't fair! You know I cain't abide seein' a woman cry.

NELLIE BESS: I'm not much concerned about what you can or cannot "abide."

(She produces a tissue, wipes her eyes and blows her nose; THURMOND half-heartedly nibbles at popcorn, alternating between sneaking looks at her and the movie screen.)

NELLIE BESS: If that damned old movie's so much more important than I am, go ahead and turn it up.

THURMOND *(quickly)*: Aw, I ain't payin' it no mind. Honest.

NELLIE BESS *(flatly)*: Of course not.

THURMOND (*after a beat*): Come here, Hon.

(*He reaches for her and pulls her to his side; she permits it, though doing little to assist him.* THURMOND *snuggles her but looks straight ahead, as if at the movie screen.*)

THURMOND: Lissen, darlin', I really and truly been thinkin' about thangs. But, Nellie Bess, we cain't gallop off to Nashville and live in a open field and eat bush-berries until we get ourselves set up! You know I ain't got a dime, and *your* money's bein' gobbled up ever' day you pay rent in that old mo-tel. I've wracked my brain tryin' to figger a way, but I cain't come up with a sensible answer. It's not that I ain't tried, or that I don't care!

NELLIE BESS (*pulling back to look at him*): I've said it before . . . Gus is your best shot.

THURMOND: Aw, I dunno. One day you might think Gus would sprang for a thousand dollars and the next day you know he wouldn't turn a-loose of forty-fie cents. He's as changeable as the wind.

NELLIE BESS: He likes us both. I think he'd be inclined to help.

THURMOND: He likes you a lot better'n he likes me.

NELLIE BESS: Thurmond, *I* can't ask him. If Gus thought you'd sent me to him, he'd be so outraged he'd dig in his heels. (*A beat.*) Besides, this wonderful state has a law that no married woman can borrow money or even buy on credit without her husband's signature. And can't you see Howard happily cosigning a note so I can take you to Nashville? Especially now that my good Christian mama has written him, hinting strongly that he should come get me before it's too late.

THURMOND (*alarmed*): Goddamn! She done that?

NELLIE BESS: She left me a note at the motel, saying she had. For my "own good"?

THURMOND: Oh shit. *(A beat.)* He very high-tempered? Your husband?

NELLIE BESS: *Thurmond!* . . . It's time to fish or cut bait. Time to show a little backbone, Thurmond. Nothing worthwhile is without some risk! If you can't risk having your feelings hurt, for a chance to start a new life with at least a *hint* of promise . . . well, then, I'd say you deserve to stay here and turn to a rock.

(She moves a bit away from him.)

THURMOND *(reaching for her hand)*: Nellie Bess . . . there's one thang I hadn't wanted to mention.

(She looks at him quizzically.)

See, Gus ain't likely to put up a nickel if he thinks it's goin' to the cause of me and you takin' off together. He . . . thinks I'm all wrong for you.

(NELLIE BESS moves back to him, reaches up and runs a hand through his hair.)

NELLIE BESS *(softly)*: I think I'm woman enough to decide what's right or wrong for me . . . don't you?

(She lightly kisses him. He embraces her and returns the kiss.)

NELLIE BESS: Tomorrow?

THURMOND: Whut?

NELLIE BESS: Will you ask Gus tomorrow?

(*THURMOND squirms but does not answer. She kisses him again.*)

NELLIE BESS: Tomorrow, baby?

THURMOND (*after a beat*): Okay. Tomorrow.

(*She rewards him with a passionate kiss, and while doing so reaches over to turn the speaker back on. Again we hear the sounds of battle. NELLIE BESS smiles at THURMOND, moves slightly apart and reaches for his popcorn. She sits looking at the movie, nibbling popcorn, a half-smile on her face while THURMOND moves and shuffles restlessly in his seat. Lights dim to . . .*)

BLACKOUT

Act II/Scene 3

From the dark we hear a country-western love ballad. The lights come up on the final two lines of the song. At lights up, THUR-MOND *is seen in his scruffy cowboy clothes, sitting alone at the domino table while drinking a bottle of beer. A pint of bourbon, uncapped, sits on the table;* THURMOND's *guitar rests in a nearby chair.* GUS, *behind the bar, is reading a newspaper spread out on the bar.*

GUS (*at end of song*): You ever git the feelin' the same damn news is printed in the paper ever' day? (*A beat.*) This-many people killed in that-many car wrecks. This-many oil wells spudded in and that-many plugged. So-many killed in Korea and so-many wounded. (*A beat.*) I read the paper for nearly a hour the other day before noticin' the goddamn thing was four months old.

THURMOND (*rising and approaching bar*): Uh . . . Gus?

GUS: Yeah?

(THURMOND *shuffles uncertainly; he can't bring himself to ask for getaway money. He fishes out a dollar.*)

THURMOND: Gimme some more jukebox coins.

GUS (*turning a page*): The jukebox is closed.

THURMOND: Whatta ya mean the jukebox is closed? I been playin' it all afternoon.

GUS: That's precisely why it's now closed.

THURMOND: You . . . you cain't just close down a public juke-box without any warnin'! Why, hailfar, I bet there's some state *law* against closin' down the only goddamn jukebox in town in the middle of the day!

GUS *(tossing aside newspaper)*: Well there oughta be a law against anybody havin' to suffer a half-a-day of them she-crapped-on-me songs, unless he's got a broke heart of his own. *(A beat.)* Didn't your pal Hank Williams ever git any nookie that didn't go bad on him?

THURMOND: You oughta be ashamed of that cheap shot! All them songs was wrote to Hank's wife, Miss Audrey, when him and her was split up and he was hurtin' bad! Hank wrote them songs from his gut!

GUS *(grinning)*: No wonder they sound a little bilious.

THURMOND: A old limp-lizard like you probably ain't ever had a heart to break.

  (He starts to walk away, then thinks of a real zinger to put GUS *in his place, and turns back.)*

You just a goddamn . . . Philippine!

GUS: A . . . *what?*

THURMOND *(thinking it over)*: I mean a . . . Palestinian!

  (He crosses to his table, sits and takes a big swig from his whis-key bottle. GUS *regards him with a mixture of perplexity and amusement.)*

GUS: Why you been mopin' around the last few days? I figgered you'd be struttin' proud after gettin' Nellie Bess tossed out of her mama's house.

THURMOND: She wadn't tossed out. She moved out on her own.

GUS: Yeah. And the whole damn town knows what was at the bottom of it.

THURMOND: I ain't responsible for what the damn town knows.

GUS: Well who *is* responsible, the Weather Bureau? My God, Thurmond, you and that girl has been about as discreet as two old street dogs.

THURMOND: We was gettin' along fine until the gossips started stirrin' shit. (*A beat.*) Now she's livin' in that crummy mo-tel . . . cryin' half the time, nippin' at my ass the rest of the time. I hafta sneak around like a goddamn burglar to even *see* her! And then she ain't herself. (*A beat.*) She's . . . by God, Gus, she's even threatenin' to run off to Fort Worth or Austin or maybe even New York! What in the hail would she do in *New York*? She don't even speak a foreign language!

GUS: If you care about that gal, you'll do all you can to help her move on. Now if *you* wanta set around here on your butt 'til it rots a pound at a time, I reckon that's your bidness. But encouragin' her to stay here is another kinda crime.

THURMOND (*rising, crossing to the bar*): Who appointed you God? Who put you in charge of Nellie Bess's life? What *is* it with you? You got some kinda crazy old man's crush on her, or what?

(GUS *turns away and occupies himself with small busywork.*)

By God, that's *it*, ain't it? I'll be a suck-egg mule! Here you been

posin' as some sorta sweet old uncle to her and all the time . . .
Shhh! Well eat your heart out, you old fool. You got the same
chance with Nellie Bess I got to wake up tomorrow mornin' a goddamn millionaire! Oh, a lotta thangs about you are comin' clear to
me now!

G U S (*sharply*): Ain't one thing in the world clear to you, you silly
young jackass! What you know about life and people could be put
in a thimble and still have room to rattle around.

T H U R M O N D: I see through *you* good enough!

G U S (*calmer*): Sure, I got a warm spot for that girl. It don't take a
genius to see that. I spotted her a long time ago as one of the few
kids passin' through this dungpile that might be bright enough
and lucky enough to escape it without carryin' its stink the rest of
her life. Yeah, Thurmond, you could say I love her . . . and hope
for her . . . in ways you never will be able to understand.

 (T H U R M O N D *shuffles uncertainly.*)

So go ahead and laugh at this old fool. Only maybe ever' now and
again you oughta stop to think about who the joke is on.

 (G U S *picks up a cloth, walks away a few steps and begins to
 polish the bar, talking as if to himself.*)

Kids! You damn kids think you'll always be young and slim and
good-lookin' and that tomorrows will stretch out before you as far
as you can see. And that somewhere out there'll always be a rain-
bow and a big rock-candy mountain.

 (*He stops polishing and looks directly at* T H U R M O N D .)

Well take a look at me. (*A beat.*) Goddammit, boy, I said *look* at me!

(THURMOND *reluctantly does so.*)

Take a *good* look. I used to be young and slim and good-lookin' myself. (*A beat.*) And how many goddamn tomorrows or rainbows or big rock-candy mountains you think is ahead of me?

THURMOND (*subdued; embarrassed*): Aw, hail, Gus . . . I wadn't really accusin' you of nothin'.

(*After a long beat,* GUS *takes a coin from his pocket and flips it to* THURMOND.)

GUS: Here, go on and play the damn jukebox. I'm through singin' my sad old song.

THURMOND (*hesitating, then placing the coin on the bar*): I'd . . . really druther sing you a song of my own.

GUS: Well . . . I reckon I left myself wide open for that 'un.

THURMOND: I got a purpose, Gus. (*Crossing to his guitar.*) We can talk about it after you hear it.

(THURMOND *gets his guitar, sits, and starts strumming as* GUS *lights a cigarette and leans against the bar to listen.*)

THURMOND (*singing*):

> Yesterday seemed too early
> But now tomorrow's too late
> Ain't no doubt
> My bad timin'
> Decided my fay-aaate . . .
> If I'd just said "I love you"

Today I'd be . . . with sweet Kate
But yesterday seemed too early
And now tomorrow's too late.

(Short guitar interlude.)

Yesterday seemed too early
But now tomorrow's too late
Once my load
Seemed much lighter
And I could pull my own weight . . .
If I'd played my cards smarter
I mighta filled . . . that big straight
But yesterday seemed too early
And . . . now . . . tomorrow's . . .
Too late . . .

(THURMOND *hits his guitar a concluding riff and looks at*
GUS, *who continues silently smoking.*)

THURMOND: Well . . .? (*A long beat.*) You still awake?

GUS: I've heard worse songs. And some of 'em wadn't even yours.

THURMOND (*grinning*): Comin' from you that's a rave review!

GUS: By the time you git through tellin' it, I'll probably be accused of nominatin' that song for the Hit Parade.

(THURMOND *rises and crosses quickly to the bar.*)

THURMOND (*eagerly*): Gus, them two new songs? Well I got big plans for 'em. I been thinkin' of takin' 'em to Nashville and tryin' to peddle 'em personal.

GUS: Now *there's* a tune I've heard many a time.

T H U R M O N D: This ain't beer talk or dream talk, Gus, I mean it this time! See, just mailin' songs to Nashville ain't worked out. So I thought I'd change my luck by goin' down there and puttin' on the hustle.

G U S (*regarding him levelly*): And this time you wouldn't have to face the big world all by your lonesome. Right?

T H U R M O N D: Well, I . . . wanted to talk to you about that part.

G U S: I think I need a beer to hear it.

(*He produces two beers and opens them as* T H U R M O N D *makes his pitch.*)

T H U R M O N D: See, Gus, Nellie Bess is gonna git a office job to help out. We figger she might hook on with one a them big music publishin' houses in Nashville, see, where she could gimme a push from the inside? We've thought this thang out real good.

G U S: Shit! You ain't thinkin' a-tall. You're livin' some bad movie in your mind.

T H U R M O N D: What's wrong with our plan?

G U S: Half the kids that own guitars is in Nashville and the other half's plannin' to go! And likely *their* wives or girlfriends thought of gettin' a "inside job" with a music company long before the notion struck you or Nellie Bess.

T H U R M O N D: We ain't afraida the challenge!

G U S: She'll wind up slingin' hash to pay the rent on some flophouse room and you'll butt your head against ever' door in Nashville without openin' one by a crack. You'll both wind up with your hearts broke and blamin' each other and with nowheres to go.

THURMOND: Folks has done it before! Nobody was *borned* a famous songwriter.

GUS: Yeah, but for ever' son-of-a-buck that makes it, they ship home a boatload of failures. I'm talkin' percentages, son. I'm talkin' reality.

THURMOND: Well for damn sure I won't never make it if I don't try! You . . . you musta told me that a thousand times yourownself!

GUS: Not about Nashville I didn't! I've always talked about you gettin' a good payin' job, maybe learnin' a good trade and buildin' for the long haul.

THURMOND: You know what "the long haul" gits you, Gus? Same as it got my daddy. Big sweat and little dollars. And a long haul to the cemetery when a gas well blowed out and he got killed in the rig far. I ain't lookin' for *that* in my future!

GUS: Whose bright idea is this Nashville trip?

THURMOND: Well. We both want it. Me and Nellie Bess.

GUS: But she's the one pushin' it?

THURMOND *(patiently)*: She wouldn't *be* pushin' it if she didn't have faith in me and my songs.

GUS: Goddammit, Thurmond, back off and look past the end of your nose! That girl's situation is so desperate she might put her faith in fairies and leprechauns.

THURMOND *(quietly, and after a long beat)*: We need a loan, Gus. Whatever you can spare. To stake us to a chance.

GUS: Thurmond, now—

THURMOND: I swear we'll pay you back! Even if Nellie Bess has to . . . take in washin' and ironin' and I hafta climb oil rigs and clank pig iron 'til I'm as old as you are!

GUS: I'm satisfied you mean that, son. But there's several reasons I can't do it. Without goin' any deeper into it, the main one is . . . what it'd wind up doin' to Nellie Bess.

THURMOND (*hotly*): For somebody that claims to be so crazy about her, you sure don't seem to have much faith in her!

GUS: I got all the faith in the world in her. I just can't have much faith in her judgment right now.

(THURMOND *slumps against the bar in defeat.*)

THURMOND: If that's your final answer.

(*A long beat.*)

Never mind. Forget it.

(*He rapidly exits.*)

GUS: Hey! You ain't even touched your free beer!

(THURMOND, *not responding, exits.*)

GUS (*calling after him*): You even forgot your damn guitar.

BLACKOUT

Act II/Scene 4

Hours later, the middle of the night. We hear night sounds: crickets, perhaps a dog howling, a truck grinding from far off. Dim lights come up on the Sundowner. The barroom is deserted and shows the debris of the night's trade. Upstairs, GUS *is asleep in the gloom of his room. Then, suddenly, a god-awful noise: someone repeatedly and desperately pounding on the door of the beer joint. We hear,* VO, THURMOND's *panicky voice.*

THURMOND(*offstage*): Gus! Open up! Gus! Let me in, Gus!

(GUS *rushes downstairs. As he comes down the stairs, he flicks a light switch, bringing barroom lights up, and continues rushing for the door as the pounding and yelling continue almost constantly.*)

GUS (*crossing*): Don't knock the damn hinges off!

(*But the noise continues until* GUS *unbolts and opens the door;* THURMOND, *in his usual cowboy outfit, almost knocks* GUS *down as he rushes in while babbling nonstop.*)

THURMOND (*scared witless*): Oh my God, Gus, you ain't gonna believe what's happened! You got to hide me!

(*He grabs* GUS *and continues his nonstop babbling.*)

I think I killed him! My God, I didn't *go* to do it! You gotta believe that and you gotta help me git away.

GUS: Calm down! Calm down! Tell me what's the trouble!

THURMOND: Shut that door, Gus! Turn out the lights!

(THURMOND *runs to the middle of the barroom, still in a frenzy, wildly looking about.*)

Where's the damn light switch?

GUS: On the stairs. *What's goin' on?*

(THURMOND *rushes behind the bar and to the stairs; he flips the light switch, and downstairs lights go dim as confused crosstalk occurs.*)

THURMOND: Shut that damn   GUS: Pull yourself together!
door and lock it!

Oh shit, Gus, I need a drink!
I gotta have a drink!

(GUS *slams the door shut but does* not *lock it as* THURMOND *fumbles with getting a beer open; he takes a beer hit as* GUS *rapidly crosses toward the bar.*)

GUS (*crossing*): Now what the hell have you *done?*

THURMOND: Oh my God, it couldn't possibly be no worse! I didn't go to kill him, Gus, honest to God I didn't!

GUS: *Kill who?*

THURMOND (*babbling on*): I went in there to take money to pay our way to Nashville, I admit that, but I was gonna pay it back! And he was drivin' by and seen my flashlight shinin' in the office and he come in with a big pistol in his hand and caught me tryin' to open the safe—

GUS: *Who?* The Sheriff?

THURMOND: *No! Tood Brandon!* Tood bragged he'd send my ass to the State Pen, Gus, and I tried to talk him out of it but he wouldn't lissen—

GUS: How'd you hurt him? Did ya *shoot* him?

THURMOND (*still babbling*): —and he kept on sayin' he was gonna put me in the pen for twenny years, Gus, and that niggers would screw me and guards would beat my ass to blubber and I lost my head and punched him out! Not to kill, Gus, I swear to Christ!

GUS: You sure he's dead?

THURMOND: Oh shit, Gus, he went down like a ton a damn bricks! His head hit the floor and made a poppin' sound and blood spurted everwhurs—

(THURMOND *can't go on; he begins sobbing: deep, wracking sobs; he pounds the top of the bar.*)

GUS: Did you check his pulse or to see if he was breathin'?

THURMOND (*still sobbing*): Shit, Gus, I . . . just . . . *run!*

GUS: Then he might still be alive! I'll call and git a doctor over there.

(GUS *starts to cross to the lift-up panel to go behind the bar, but* THURMOND *suddenly leaps and grabs the shotgun on the gun rack behind the bar. He quickly pumps a shell into the chamber and points it at* GUS.)

THURMOND: No! Stop!

GUS (*stopping dead still*): Don't be a damn fool, Boy!

THURMOND: I ain't goin' to no State Pen, Gus!

GUS: If Tood ain't dead, somethin' can be worked out!

THURMOND: He's dead! I hit him a hell of a shot!

GUS: Put the shotgun down, Boy.

THURMOND: Don't make me hurt you, Gus.

GUS: Easy. Stand easy, Son.

THURMOND: I gotta run and hide! You gimme the money!

GUS: We don't know for sure that Tood's dead. Now if you'll let me call and get help, I can testify that you come here for that purpose.

THURMOND: They'll lock my ass up, Gus.

GUS: We'll get a lawyer and bail you out! Tood had a gun and threatened you, so you hit him in self-defense.

THURMOND: Won't nobody believe that.

GUS: They might if it's told right.

THURMOND: Not when it comes out I went to rob him.

GUS: Now, calm down and think—had you got the safe open before Tood came in with the gun?

THURMOND: Naw, I was nervous and—

GUS: Then I don't see no damn robbery.

THURMOND: But what'll I claim I was doin' there in the middle of the night?

THURMOND: We'll get some hotshot Odessa lawyer who'll prob'ly be able to figure things out a lot better than they mighta happened. But now we gotta get some medical help to Tood, and the quicker the better.

THURMOND: Oh, God, I just don't know.

GUS: Dammit, it's the only chance you got. Now, lemme get to that phone! (*A beat; softly.*) Please . . .

(THURMOND *hesitates, then lowers the gun and steps back.* GUS *brushes by him, grabs the telephone and dials the operator*).

GUS: Miss Molly? Gus Gilbert. Now, listen real careful. Ring up Doc Legg's house and— Yeah, yeah, I know it's real late, but this is an emergency— Just shut up and listen! Now, tell Doc Legg to hurry over to Tood Brandon's Gulf station. Tood's over there hurt, maybe real bad. (*To* THURMAN.) The door unlocked?

THURMOND: Yeah, when I run off—

GUS (*into phone*): Door's open at the Gulf station, the Doc can just go in! Now, *after* you get Doc on the way, Molly, call the Sheriff's office and tell 'em to get a ambulance to Tood's Gulf station.

(*The sound of a police siren is heard, coming closer.*)

THURMOND: Oh shit, Gus, they've found him! They're comin' after me!

(*He clutches* GUS *with one hand and pulls him off-balance.*)

GUS: Dammit, Thurmond! (*Into phone.*) No, Molly, you make the calls, I got my hands full here!

(*Police siren howls closer, growls to an end, and perhaps we see the glow of a flashing red light outside. Sound of a car door slamming. Confused crosstalk.*)

GUS (*into telephone*): No need to call the Sheriff's office, they're here. Just call the Doc and a ambulance. I gotta go.

THURMOND: What'll I do, Gus? They'll take me away!

Talk to 'em for me, Gus!

(*As* GUS *hangs up the phone,* SHERIFF LANDON *rushes in and they turn toward him. Seeing* THURMOND *with the shotgun in his hand, the* SHERIFF *immediately goes into a crouch and pulls his pistol.*)

GUS: *Drop the shotgun, Thurmond!*

(*But before* THURMOND *can even think of dropping the shotgun—indeed, before* GUS *has finished his line—the* SHERIFF *snaps off a quick shot at* THURMOND. *It misses him, but* THURMOND'*s reflex action is to pull the trigger of the shotgun and it goes off with a loud blast. The charge goes nowhere near the* SHERIFF, *but up toward the ceiling. The* SHERIFF *is excited, however, and fires a second time as* THURMOND *drops the shotgun and runs for the stairs.*)

GUS (*ducking and screaming*): NO NO NO!

(*But the* SHERIFF *fires two more shots and one catches* THURMOND *in the back as he is halfway up the stairs. Blood spurts as he falls.*)

THURMOND: Oh, God! *Mama!*

(THURMOND *slides partway back down the stairs as* GUS *runs to him.*)

GUS: Oh, Sweet Jesus! *Thurmond!*

(*He whirls to face the* SHERIFF.)

You killed him, you son-of-a-bitch!

SHERIFF LANDON (*excited*): Goddammit, he throwed down on me! You seen it!

GUS: *You shot him in the back when he was runnin' away, you bastard!*

(GUS *turns away and bends over* THURMOND *again, frantically searching for signs of life.*)

SHERIFF LANDON (*hurriedly and agitated*): Now dammit, when I run in here I seen him holdin' the shotgun on you and then he turned and throwed down on me! He didn't gimme any choice but to shoot him and that's the way it happened! And he'd already half-killed poor old Tood Brandon!

(*The* SHERIFF, *gun in hand still, takes measured steps toward the end of the bar nearest* THURMOND's *body as* GUS—*still kneeling—drops his head and weeps.*)

GUS (*weeping*): Goddamn . . . Goddamn . . . Goddamn . . .

BLACKOUT

Act II/Scene 5

Two days later, immediately after THURMOND's *funeral. While
in the dark, we hear the same sad song that ended Act I when*
THURMOND *and* NELLIE BESS *exchanged their first kiss
of their affair. On the last line of the song, lights come up on the
barroom of the Sundowner. For a couple of beats no actors are
onstage. We hear the street door being unlocked, then* GUS *and*
MOON *enter. They are wearing their best suits, which are neither
new nor fashionable;* MOON *wears an old felt hat with the brim
turned up all around. They move with a certain torpor, though in
the early part of the scene—after getting beers—they show the
temporary relief that surfaces once a funeral is over.*

GUS (*while crossing*): Excuse this place, Moon. Last couple a
days I hadn't had time to do much more'n mop up the blood.

MOON: Don't mention it.

(GUS *goes behind the bar, unlocks a beer cooler and produces
two beers.*)

GUS (*opening beers*): Can you think of a more pagan ritual than a
damn funeral?

MOON: I ain't ever been to one that didn't gimme the heebie-
jeebies.

(GUS *shoves a beer across to* MOON .)

GUS: Dunno why that boy's ol' mama insisted on a open casket,
him all painted up like a circus clown.

(They drink, long and deeply.)

I guess it's a way of postponin' never seein' somebody again, but if I had any say I'd outlaw it.

MOON: Lotsa folks say we'll see the dead again. In Heaven.

GUS *(giving him a look)*: You believe that?

MOON: If there's a Heaven there must be a Hell . . . so I'm kinda scared not to. *(A beat.)* You?

GUS: Naw, I hadn't had any luck makin' myself believe that . . . pie-in-the-sky stuff. I think it's just a little somethin' else to hold over people's heads and try to keep 'em in line.

(They drink.)

Know anybody inner-rested in buyin' a fourth-class beer joint?

MOON: Aw, Gus, don't be talkin' thatta-way.

GUS: I'm tempted to burn this son-of-a-buck plumb to the ground, drive off and not even look back.

MOON: You ain't goin' nowhere. This here's your home.

(GUS slaps the tabletop a sharp lick.)

GUS: None of this had to happen, goddammit!

MOON: A lotta folks is all worked-up. I hear people talkin'.

GUS *(sharply)*: Naw, you hear a buncha sheep goin' ba-ba-ba! Not one damn thing's gonna be done about a flat-out murder. *(A beat.*) Tood Brandon's already drawin' crowds, making that clumsy robbery attempt sound like it was pulled off by Jesse James or the Dalton Gang.

M O O N (*hesitant*): Well . . . Tood couldn't hardly be expected to take bein' robbed laying down.

G U S: He don't have to make a Wild West yarn out of it! And that punk Sheriff don't hafta be so quick to pose for newspaper pictures. (*A beat.*) Maybe if I hadn't kept that damn loaded shotgun on the wall . . .

M O O N: Don't go floggin' yourself. Drunk oil boomers or drunk cowboys mighta scobbed your knob many a time without that gun.

G U S: That's what I been tellin' myself. But it don't seem to help. (*A beat.*) What pisses me off is the Sheriff gettin' away with lyin' about what happened in here.

M O O N: Them courthouse suckers all stick together.

G U S: Way they see it, Thurmond got what was comin' to him. So, fuck it, sweep it under the rug. Forget it. Live happy-ever-after. (*A beat.*) If I was a little younger, or had a little more backbone, maybe I'd push and howl a little more. (*A longer beat.*) But I ain't . . . and I don't . . . and that's all she wrote.

(*They sit in silence.* N E L L I E   B E S S *enters; she is dressed in black and she stops just inside the door.*)

G U S (*rising*): Come in, Honey. Looks like you could use a cold beer.

(M O O N, *on spotting* N E L L I E   B E S S, *snatches off his hat as a mark of respect.*)

NELLIE BESS: I can't stay. Howard is . . . waiting for me. Out in the car.

GUS: Yeah. I . . . seen him at the cemetery. *(Long beat.)* Nice-lookin' man. *(Awkward pause.)* Moon, you mind?

MOON: Huh?

(GUS *gives him a stern look.* MOON *catches on, performs an uncertain shuffle step, picks up his beer to take it with him, has second thoughts, places it back down and rapidly exits.)*

NELLIE BESS: I came to say I'm sorry, Gus. I can't sleep for thinking this whole . . . nightmare . . . has been my fault.

GUS: I'm eat up with guilt myself, Honey, but I'll get over that in time. And so must you.

(NELLIE BESS *begins crying softly;* GUS *goes to her and offers his handkerchief; she takes it and dabs at her eyes.)*

NELLIE BESS *(trying to smile):* Seems you're . . . always doing this. *(A beat.)* I just remember it in some old fog . . . from when I was little. I fell on the sidewalk and skinned my knee. You picked me up . . . and wiped my eyes and blew my nose.

GUS *(remembering):* It was your first time on roller skates. *(A beat.)* When I took you home, your mama blessed me out like a drunk sailor.

NELLIE BESS: But . . . why'd she get mad at you?

GUS *(after a beat):* I'd bought the roller skates.

(They exchange a look.)

NELLIE BESS: Oh God, Gus! Maybe I pushed him too much.

GUS: I know, I know. I made a damn hobby of pushin' that boy myself. All I seen was a kid not tryin' to better hisself . . . and I didn't want him endin' up old and bogged down like me.

NELLIE BESS: I was scared of what might become of me. I saw a way out.

GUS: Don't beat up on yourself.

NELLIE BESS: But that's not all of it. I don't want you thinking—

(Offstage, a car horn beeps twice.)

Oh! Howard . . . He's in a hurry. To get back to his clinic.

GUS: Long drive to Cisco.

NELLIE BESS *(after a beat)*: Maybe I did use him, Gus, but I· really and truly *felt* something in my heart—

GUS *(cutting her off)*: Nobody blames you!

NELLIE BESS: *I* blame me. *(A beat.)* I looked at him today . . . in that awful box . . . and I hoped that, somehow, he might know the . . . regret I feel. *(A beat.)* Regret that I didn't say more about the good I knew to be in him . . . and his talent . . . and his sweet, foolish trust.

*(*GUS *looks away.)*

You know his real "crime," Gus?

(He looks at her.)

He was a dreamer . . . in a dreamless land.

G U S: It's done. Now . . . just . . . get through it.

(Offstage, the car horn beeps three times.)

N E L L I E   B E S S: I'll write you a letter . . .

G U S: You do that.

(Offstage, the car horn issues four short, angry beeps.)

N E L L I E   B E S S: My master's voice . . .

(They hold a long look. Then G U S goes quickly toward her. She comes to meet him. They embrace tightly.)

G U S: Take care of yourself, Darlin'. *(A beat.)* This old world wouldn't be the same without you.

(N E L L I E   B E S S suddenly breaks the embrace, turns and rushes through the door; offstage the car horn beeps incessantly until she has exited. G U S stares after her for a moment, takes a couple of steps as if to follow, then stops. He stands motionless for a moment. Suddenly, he kicks a chair, sending it scooting across the floor. This act lets loose his demons, sends him into a destructive frenzy. He knocks over chairs, tables, beer bottles, whatever is in his path, and finally slumps over the bar where he breathes heavily for several beats. When he straightens up from the bar he looks dumbly at the havoc he has wrought, then slowly moves around picking up a chair . . . a bottle . . . until he suddenly stops, drops the bottle, and slumps heavily into the chair he has set up. He puts his head in his hands for a few beats, then breaks into wracking sobs. When he controls them, he raises his head and stares emptily into space. We hear V O I C E   O V E R—softly at first, growing ever-stronger—the

voice of T H U R M O N D *singing a verse of his song "Tomorrow's Too Late.")*

T H U R M O N D (V O):

> Yesterday seemed too early
> But now tomorrow's too late
> Ain't no doubt
> My bad timin'
> Decided my fay-aaate . . .
> If I'd played my cards smarter
> I mighta filled . . . that big straight
> But yesterday seemed too early
> And now tomorrow's too late.

(Lights, which started slowly dimming as the song began, continue the process as we see G U S *staring off into the distance in the increasing gloom.)*

T H U R M O N D (V O):

> Yesterday seemed . . . too early . . .
> And now tomorrow's . . .
> Too . . . late. . . .

B L A C K O U T

and

T H E   E N D

Credit and Thanks

For Helping to Develop *The Night Hank Williams Died*

Workshop Production: At Memphis State University, November 15–19, 1985. Directed by Keith Kennedy. Stage Manager: Tricia Warren. Production Staff: Oliver Hinson, Johnnie Ferrell, Ellen Caldwell, Terry Scott and Jim West. *Cast:* Thurmond Stottle: Mark W. Johnson; Gus Gilbert: Jim Palmer; Nellie Bess Powers Clark: Stacey May; Moon Childers: Ken Parnell; Sheriff Royce Landon: James A. West; Mrs. Vida Powers: Joanna Helming; Radio Voice: Bob McDowell. (The roles of Sugarbugger and Frank Klapproth, a couple of Ohio tourists later written out of the play, were played in Memphis by Deirdre Hade and John McCormack, respectively.)

First Professional Production: At New Playwrights' Theatre, Washington, D.C. February 2–March 6, 1988. Directed by Peter Frisch. Stage Manager: John Lescault. Set Design: Clifton R. Welch. Lighting Design: Daniel MacLean Wagner. Costume Design: Jeffrey Ullman. *Cast:* Thurmond Stottle: Mark W. Johnson; Gus Gilbert: Larry L. King; Nellie Bess Powers Clark: Elizabeth DuVall; Moon Childers: Grady Smith; Sheriff Royce Landon, Jr.: Gregory Procaccino; Mrs. Vida Powers: Janis Benson; Radio Voice: James H. Boren.

Original Texas Producton: At Live Oak Theatre, Austin, September 16–November 5, 1988. Directed by Don Toner. Stage Manager: Lou Rigler. Set Design: Jim Carroccio. Lighting Design: Ken Hudson. Sound Design: Bruce Truitt. Costume Design: Susan Branch. *Cast:* Thurmond Stottle: Gabriel Folse; Gus Gilbert: Lou Perry; Nellie Bess Powers Clark: Christine Poole; Moon Childers: Grady Smith; Sheriff Royce Landon, Jr.: Ev Lunning, Jr.; Mrs. Vida Powers: Jill Parker-Jones; Radio Voice: Sammy Allred.

First New York Production: At Off-Broadway WPA Theatre in Manhattan, January 24–February 26, 1989. Directed by Christopher Ashley. Stage Manager: Greta Minsky. Set Design: Edward T. Gianfrancesco. Lighting Design: Craig Evans. Sound Design: Aural Fixation. Costume Design: Jess Goldstein. Resident Artistic Director: Kyle Renick. *Cast:* Thurmond Stottle: Matt Mulhern; Gus Gilbert: Barton Heyman; Nellie Bess Powers Clark: Betsy Aidem; Moon Childers: J. R. Horne; Sheriff Royce Landon, Jr.: Steve Rankin; Mrs. Vida Powers: Phyllis Somerville; Radio Voice: Larry L. King.*

*The same cast, with the exception of Darren McGavin as Gus, Grady Smith as Moon and Earl Hindman as the Sheriff, opened at the Orpheum Theatre in New York on March 31, 1989, for an open-ended run produced by Drew Dennett.